HIGHLIGHTS OF THE
CARY GRAPHIC ARTS COLLECTION

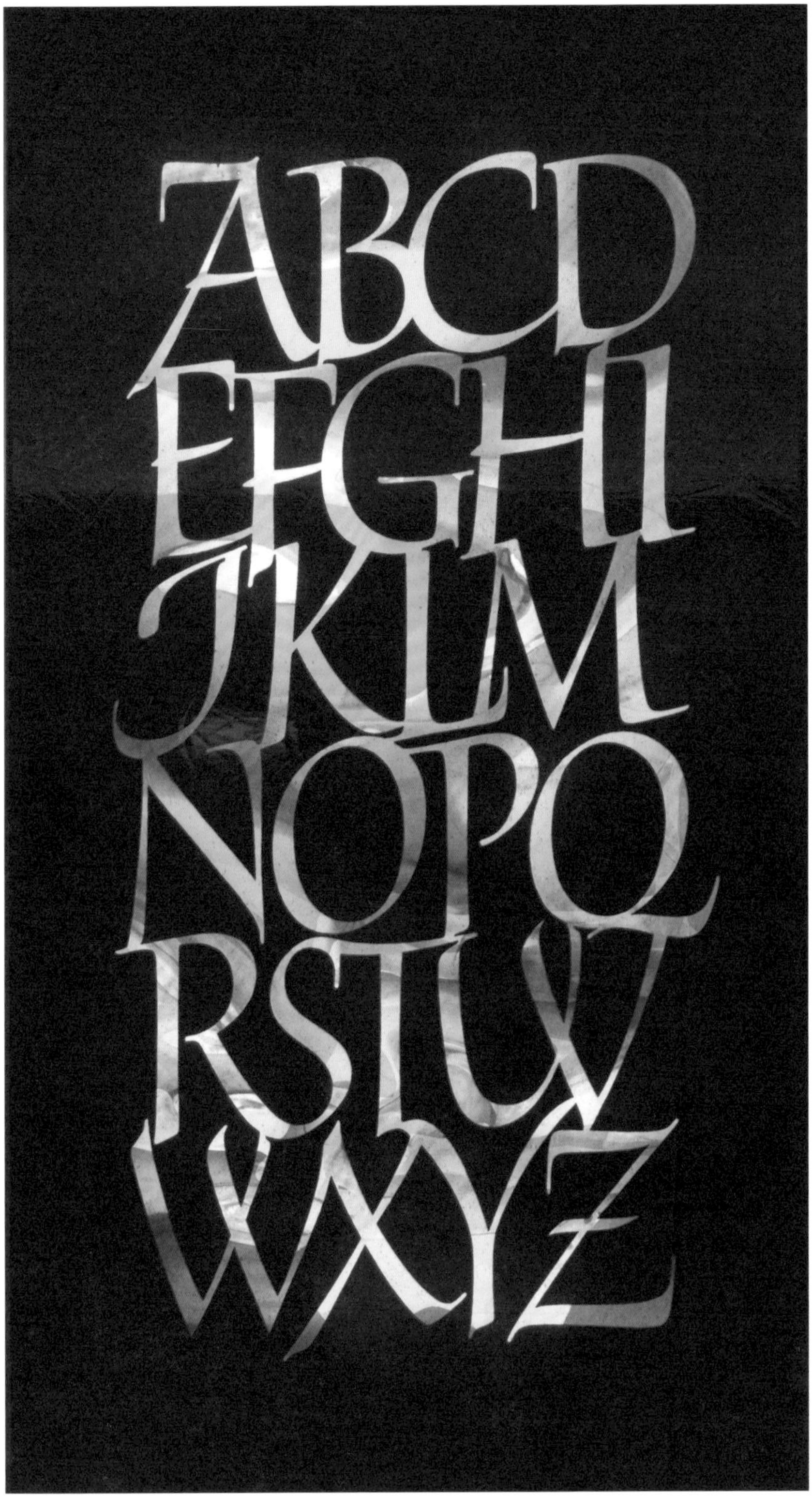
ABCD
EFGHI
JKLM
NOPQ
RSTUV
WXYZ

HIGHLIGHTS OF THE
CARY GRAPHIC ARTS COLLECTION
at Rochester Institute of Technology

Steven K. Galbraith
Amelia Hugill-Fontanel
Kari Horowicz

RIT Press
Rochester, New York

RIT Press
90 Lomb Memorial Drive
Rochester, New York 14623-5604
http://ritpress.rit.edu

Cover image:
Frontispiece: Stained glass designed by Julian Waters and created by
Valerie Murray Stained Glass Studio.

Designed by Marnie Soom
Printed in the U.S.A.
ISBN 978-1-939125-13-2

Library of Congress Cataloging-in-Publication Data

Rochester Institute of Technology.
    Highlights of the Cary Graphic Arts Collection at Rochester Institute of
Technology / Steven K. Galbraith, Amelia Hugill-Fontanel, Kari Horowicz.
        pages   cm
    Includes index.
    ISBN 978-1-939125-13-2 (alk. paper)
1. Graphic design (Typography)—Catalogs. 2. Graphic arts—Catalogs.
3. Melbert B. Cary, Jr. Graphic Arts Collection—Catalogs. I.
Galbraith, Steven Kenneth, author. II. Hugill-Fontanel, Amelia, 1975–
author. III. Horowicz, Kari, 1961– author. IV. Title.
    Z246.R59 2014
    741.6074'74789–dc23
                                                    2014037562

CONTENTS

INTRODUCTION

"THE TYPE SPEAKS"

During the hours in which the Cary Graphic Arts Collection is open, light from a stained-glass calligraphic alphabet radiates through the front doors into the exhibition space. This colorful alphabet was designed by Julian Waters and transformed into illuminated stained glass by Valerie Murray Stained Glass Studio. Although they were installed in the far wall of the library's reading room, the letters shine outward like a beacon, visible to those who approach or pass, drawing visitors to the library.

Waters' calligraphy is a fitting welcome. The Cary Graphic Arts Collection at Rochester Institute of Technology is one of the world's premier libraries of graphic communication history and practices. Letterforms are the foundation of graphic communication, and a focus of the Cary Collection. Waters' alphabet broadcasts our library's mission, announcing that one is about to enter a space where "the medium is the message,"[1] and "the type speaks." In fact, facing the stained glass calligraphy on the opposite side of the reading room is a sculpture by type designer Hermann Zapf honoring one of his inspirations: American type designer Frederic Goudy. Goudy's initials "FWG" are intertwined with the words "The Type Speaks." The words allude to a broadside first composed and printed by Goudy for his Village Press in 1931. Sometimes referred to by its opening line, "I am Type," Goudy's text recounts the antecedents of printing and, in doing so, summarizes the earliest forms of written communication:

> I am TYPE! Of my earliest ancestry neither history nor relics remain. The wedge-shaped symbols impressed in plastic clay in the dim past by Babylonian builders foreshadowed me. From them through the hieroglyphs of the ancient Egyptians, the lapidary

---

1 Marshall McLuhan, *Understanding Media; the Extensions of Man* (New York: McGraw-Hill, 1964), 7.

1

inscriptions of the early Romans, down to the beautiful letters by the scribes of the Italian Renaissance, I was in the making. John Gutenberg was the first to cast me in metal. From his chance thought straying through an idle reverie—a dream most golden—the profound art of printing with movable types was born.[2]

Melbert B. Cary Jr.

The long history chronicled in brief by Goudy is an evolution that is regularly on display in the Cary Collection. The past is ever present in our reading room—for example, the "wedge-shaped symbols" of three cuneiform tablets aged over 4,000 years rest in an exhibition case at the front of the room (page 18). Beside the tablets in the case are two fragments from the Egyptian *Book of the Dead* (c. 1500 BCE) showing examples of both "the hieroglyphs of the ancient Egyptians" and its contemporary hieratic script. Hanging nearby on the front wall of the library is American calligrapher Edward Catich's rubbing of the text inscribed on the base of Trajan's Column in Rome. The capital roman letters carved into this monument to the Roman emperor Trajan in 113 CE are an example of "the lapidary inscriptions of the early Romans" and would serve as exemplars for future type designers such as Goudy (page 58). "Beautiful letters by the scribes of the Italian Renaissance" are found in our collection among a selection of manuscript leaves dating from the around the early 10th century to the late 16th century. These leaves are often used as examples for RIT students who are studying calligraphy, type design, and graphic design.

Type's ancestry culminates with the advent of printing and the introduction of metal moveable type, a technology originally invented in China (page 20), but popularized in Europe beginning the mid-1450s (page 22). The Cary Collection owns two leaves from the Gutenberg Bible. These leaves are often on display, demonstrating how Johann or "John" Gutenberg repurposed the tools of metallurgists and the presses found in trades like winemaking to develop a system of casting alphabets of metal type and printing them with a press. Throughout the rest of the 15th century, printers in Gutenberg's wake would continue to refine and standardize the art of printing. Books printed during this era are referred to as incunabula, or books "from the cradle." The Cary Collection has examples of books produced by the most important printers of this period, such as Gutenberg's apprentice, Peter Schöffer (page 56), and the famous Venetian printer, Aldus Manutius (page 30). In the centuries that followed,

---

2   Quoted from *Looking Closer 3: Classic Writings on Graphic Design.* Ed. by Michael Bierut [et al.] (New York: Allworth Press: American Institute of Graphic Arts, 1999), 35.

The Cary Collection
Exhibition Gallery.

Gutenberg's inventions would spread around the world.

Measured in time, this early history spans roughly 4,500 years. The events that followed cover only about 550 years. Yet the technological advances made over the course of these five centuries are as numerous as they are profound. These are the centuries in which printing reigned as the most vital form of graphic communication, and the centuries that are the most comprehensively included in the Cary Collection.

MELBERT B. CARY JR.

The Cary Graphic Arts Collection would not exist without the spirit of Melbert B. Cary Jr. (1892–1941) and the generosity of his wife Mary Flagler Cary. Melbert Cary's life revolved around printing. He worked as director of Continental Type Founders Association, an agency that imported metal printing type from Europe to America for sale to printers. However, Cary didn't just import and sell type—he used it. He ran his own private printing press called the Press of the Woolly Whale. This fanciful name suggests the lighthearted kinds of work that the press often produced, such as *The Devil's Bible* (1933) and *The Missing Gutenberg Wood Blocks* (1940).

Cary's press was also a social hub visited by many of his friends and colleagues, all of whom are recorded in a visitors' book that is now preserved in the Cary Collection (see page 14). The 600 signatures in the book are a powerful reminder of Cary's active life in the printing and graphic design worlds. Although it captures only visitors to Cary's press from 1928–1941, the visitors' book seems to encapsulate all the players in his era's graphic design universe. Indeed, the names read almost like a partial catalog of the artists and designers present in the Cary Collection.

Cary also had a keen interest in the history of printing, and assembled a library of about 2,300 books on the subject. This included printer's manuals, type specimens, and exemplars of the printer's art. His library of printing-related books would become the foundation for the Cary Graphic Arts Collection.

THE CARY GRAPHIC ARTS COLLECTION AT ROCHESTER INSTITUTE OF TECHNOLOGY

The founding of the Cary Graphic Arts collection took place on October 9, 1969, when Melbert Cary's library was installed in RIT's School of Printing on the first floor of James E. Booth Hall. His collection was donated to RIT by the Mary Flagler Cary Charitable Trust, established earlier that year in memory of Cary's widow, who had passed away in 1967. A combination of serendipity and the vision of Alexander Lawson and Herbert Johnson of the School of Printing, and Alfred L. Davis, Vice President of Development, brought the Trust into contact with RIT.[3] The Cary trustees recognized the School of Printing's commitment to fine printing and its connections to Cary's friend, Frederic Goudy (at that time, printing students were trained in the Goudy/Coggeshall Workshop which included equipment described below). The Trust established the Cary Graphic Arts Collection at RIT in honor of Melbert Cary with the donation of his library and eventually an endowment to help run it. In addition, the Trust would establish the Cary Professorship and the annual Frederic W. Goudy Distinguished Lecture in Typography, which included an award to be presented to an exceptional typographer.

In the decades following the establishment of the Cary Collection, Cary Professors and curators continued to build upon Melbert Cary's collection, expanding the scope from the art of printing to the greater history of graphic communication. Forty-five years later, the initial collection of 2,300

---

3   Alexander S. Lawson, *The School of Printing, Rochester Institute of Technology: The First Half-Century 1937–1987* (Rochester, NY: School of Printing Management and Sciences, Rochester Institute of Technology, 1987), 283–84, 340, and 345–46.

The Cary Collection
Reading Room.

books has grown to a library of over 45,000 volumes, along with related archives. The location of the library changed as well. In 1991, while under the direction of Curator David Pankow, the Cary Collection was relocated to the second floor of the Wallace Center, allowing the library to expand its outreach, teaching, and collections. The Cary Collection is now a part of the RIT Libraries.

In the library's current space, over five hundred years of history is distilled into a collection of books shelved in glass cabinets around the perimeter of our reading room. The books range from the oldest printed book in our collection (page 56) to examples of contemporary artists' books that reimagine the book and the endless possibilities of its form (pages 16, 78). Cary Curators continue to build the collection, acquiring works that serve as exemplars of some aspect of book production, whether it be type design, printing, illustration, or bookbinding.

THE NEW YORK TIMES MUSEUM OF THE RECORDED WORD
The initial donation of Melbert Cary Jr.'s library would be followed by many important donations that have expanded the scope and mission of the

Cary Graphic Arts Collection. For example, a number of the artifacts documenting the early history of graphic communication came to the library through a generous donation from a source that some might find unlikely.

From 1938 to 1982, *The New York Times* hosted a permanent exhibition called *The New York Times* Museum of the Recorded Word. The exhibition was situated on the tenth floor of the Times Annex on West 43rd Street and open six days a week to the public.[4] In 1984, the museum was formally donated to the Cary Graphic Arts Collection. The museum's collection documents the long history of written communication, with, as you might guess, an emphasis on printed news. The scope of the collection is quite wide, beginning with ancient cuneiform tablets and ending with the printing of *The New York Times* in 1969 when Apollo astronauts landed on the moon. As Cary Curator David Pankow noted at the time, "The addition of the *Times* collection brings us back to the third millennium B.C. and certainly widens our scope." Artifacts donated by *The New York Times* featured in this catalog include cuneiform tablets (page 18), a pamphlet from c. 1470–71 that scholars consider to be the first instance of printed news (page 34), an early woodcut used for illustration (page 26), and an English hornbook c. 1600 (page 38).

The smallest artifacts to come from the museum are two pieces of metal printing type likely from Korea, c. 1400 (page 20). Although each measures less than an inch, their historical significance is massive. In the bigger picture, they are living reminders of the earliest printing executed with moveable type. At a local level they are the earliest examples pertaining to what may be the Cary Collection's deepest research strength—typography.

TYPOGRAPHY

Preserved within the Cary Collection are books containing some of the finest typography in the history of printing. These include the first italic types of Aldus Manutius (page 30), the transformative letters of Giambattista Bodoni (page 46) and the modern typographic work of Hermann Zapf (page 76). An essential part of this collection is the library's exhaustive assortment of type specimens. Beginning as early as the 16th century, type founders created catalogs of samples of their typefaces in order to increase sales to printers. Type specimens typically took the form of broadsides (posters) and books. Over the decades the Cary Collection has assembled a library of type specimens that range from a broadside of William Caslon's types from c. 1734 to specimens of typefaces designed by current RIT students. The latter is appropriate, as RIT is one of the last remaining

---

4   *The Story of the Recorded Word.* (New York Times Company: New York, 1939).

schools where a student learns type design by first studying calligraphy.

Because type specimens were essentially sales catalogs and not often saved, they tend to be ephemeral. This makes their preservation at a library like the Cary Collection all the more significant. Some type specimens rise to the level of art, such as the library's copy of a specimen of chromatic wood type, that is, wood type used to print in two or more colors. For example, a specimen printed in 1874 by the William H. Page Company, has recently attracted the attention of contemporary type designers, and will be reproduced by the Cary Collection in a facsimile edition (page 48).

The design of letters isn't limited to printing or writing on paper. What's more, "lapidary inscriptions" are not limited to the ancients. On display in the Cary Collection are several modern alphabet stones including one engraved by Eric Gill in 1938 (page 72). Gill's stone remains on permanent exhibition in the reading room, and is just one artifact related to Gill that the library owns. Along with specimens of his type (he is most famous for Gill Sans), we have many books that feature his beautiful engraved illustrations (page 66).

Book illustration and the various processes through which they were produced is another rich area of study in the Cary Collection. The first illustrations to appear in printed books were achieved using wood blocks carved in relief and printed alongside of type. The Cary Collection preserves an example of a woodcut from c. 1500 that depicts Jesus instructing his apostles (page 26). This somewhat rudimentary technology evolved into finer copper engravings, as exhibited in John Pine's engraved edition of the works of Horace (page 30) and later into wood engraving, an enduring art exemplified by the work of Barry Moser (page 28). In the 19th century, stone lithography allowed for complex multi-colored illustrations (page 50) and later evolved into modern forms of offset printing.

THE ART OF PRINTING

Elegantly designed letterforms and handsomely printed illustrations are often key ingredients for making beautiful books (along with handmade paper and fine bindings). Historically. most printers were concerned primarily with producing legible copies of texts for sale. Yet there have always been printers who produced elegant books that exemplified the art of printing. In the late 19th century, for example, William Morris extended his work in the decorative arts and crafts to book publishing as a response to the low-quality books that were being manufactured in England during the industrial age. When he printed his masterpiece *The Works of Geoffrey Chaucer* or "Kelmscott Chaucer" in 1896, he inspired generations of printers to engage in fine press printing, that is, producing books of exceptionally high quality in limited numbers.

Since the founding of the Cary Collection, fine press books have been of special interest. One of the first major acquisitions for the library was an exquisitely bound copy of the Kelmscott Chaucer (page 54). Since then, the collection of fine press printing has grown to become one of the richest and most complete. Other fine press editions here include the Cranach Press' edition of *Hamlet* (1930), considered by some to be second in quality only after the Kelmscott Chaucer, and the Pennyroyal Caxton edition of the King James Bible (1999) (page 28).

ARTHUR M LOWENTHAL MEMORIAL PRESSROOM

When it comes to documenting the history of the book and the history of printing, the Cary Collection distinguishes itself from other institutions in that the library does not only collect books, but it also collects the technology used in manufacturing books. This technology can take many forms—the Cary Collection is most passionate about the tools that were used in printing houses since the invention of printing in the West in the mid-15th century.

Bringing this history to life is our library's own print shop, the Arthur M Lowenthal Memorial Pressroom, a space that houses a collection of more than a dozen historic printing presses dating from 1820 to the 1950s. Each press is still operable and is maintained as a working press. Cary curators are active users of the presses and are often designing and printing exhibition material and other keepsakes for the Cary Collection. Student interest in letterpress printing has also inspired Cary curators to design programming in which the pressroom is open to the RIT community and general public, who are given the opportunity to print on a selection of the presses.

The Lowenthal Memorial Pressroom collection is not usually growing actively at the Cary Collection, but when the right printing press is available, we make room for it. When the Albion printing press that William Morris used to print the Kelmscott Chaucer went on auction on December 6, 2013, Cary curators acted quickly to find the means of acquiring it. Not only had the press also belonged briefly to Frederic Goudy, it spent part of its life in the print shop of Melbert B. Cary Jr. With the invaluable support of Brooks Bower, an alumnus of the School of Printing, RIT won this Albion at auction and it arrived at the Cary Collection in January 2014 (page 52).

The Kelmscott press is in good company. Standing beside it in Lowenthal Memorial Pressroom is an early 19th century Albion printing press also once owned by Frederic Goudy. This is one of the presses that Goudy used in his print shop in Marlborough on Hudson, just north of New York City. When his shop caught fire in 1939, most of his printing

equipment was damaged or destroyed. But this press was on loan to his friend Howard Coggeshall and thus spared. It eventually ended up with wood engraver John DePol, who sold it to RIT. Also on loan were stands of original printing type cast by Goudy, which Coggeshall's widow, Marie, later donated to RIT. These fonts of type are often referred to in the printing world as the "Lost Goudy Types" because the matrices (type moulds) used to cast the type were lost in the fire, thus the type can never be recast. Goudy's press and type are now preserved in the Lowenthal Memorial Pressroom and are just a part of the Cary Collection's strong assemblage of Goudyiana (page 58).

Complementing the Cary Collection's printing presses are over 1,500 fonts of metal and wood type, along with several sets of matrices used to cast famous typefaces. Part of the role of the Cary curators is to ensure that these artifacts are not only preserved for posterity, but are used more actively under the right conditions and for the right projects. For example, type designers working for companies such as Monotype, Adobe, ITC, and P22 Type Foundry have transformed our historic type and into digital fonts (page 58). What's more, the Cary Collection has collaborated with type casters to recast two typefaces: 24 pt. Centaur Capitals designed by Bruce Rogers (page 60) and Cloister Initials designed by Frederic Goudy. As a result, these fonts of metal type are available for printers for the first time in decades.

MIDDLETON COLLECTION AND BOOKBINDING

Opposite the Lowenthal Memorial Pressroom is another space in the Cary Collection dedicated to a specific aspect of the history of the book. The Dudley A. Weiss Reading Room houses the reference library of English bookbinder Bernard C. Middleton, one of the 20th century's greatest book-binders and an eminent historian of the history of the craft. The room is named for Dudley Weiss, the generous benefactor who in 1983 made possible our acquisition of Middleton's collection. The Bernard C. Middleton Collection of Books on the History and Practice of Bookbinding originally consisted of more than 2,000 volumes, and is one of the most complete collections of its kind in the world. The collection continues to grow, making bookbinding one of the Cary Collection's major research strengths.

In addition to books on bookbinding, the Middleton Collection contains archival material related to the craft, such as the bookbinding records of the Zaehnsdorf Bindery in London (1842–c.1945) and a mid 19th-century indenture outlining the conditions of a bookbinder's apprenticeship (page 40). The archive also features exemplars of fine and historic bindings, including the art of edge decoration popularized by bookbinders such as Edwards of Halifax (page 42).

AVANT-GARDE AND MODERNISM

Examples of fine and historic bookbinding are found not only in the Middleton Collection, they are present in nearly every section of the Cary Collection. Take, for example, the bolted binding adorning the master-piece of Futurism, Fortunato Depero's *Depero Futurista* from 1927 (page 64). This revolutionary book is part of the Cary's collection of avant-garde typography from the 1920s and 30s, a subject area that the library has been developing in support of interest from faculty in the School of Design. The artists represented in the avant garde collection, including the likes of Man Ray, Ladislav Sutnar, A. M. Cassandre, and El Lissitzky (page 62), radically transformed graphic design. They are the influential precursors to Modernism, the movement documented and celebrated in one of the fastest growing collections in our library, the Cary Graphic Design Archive.

In 1984, RIT Professor Roger Remington began collecting the archives of some of the 20th century's most prominent Modernist graphic designers.

Amelia Hugill-Fontanel, Associate Curator, teaching a class with photographically illustrated books from the Cary Collection. Photo by Frank Cost.

The collection began with the donation of the Lester Beall Collection, including the sketches and actualized posters he designed for the U.S. Rural Electrification Administration in the 1930s (page 80). Thirty years later, the archive has grown to a collection of over forty designers, including luminaries such as Alexey Brodovitch, Cipe Pineles, Alvin Lustig, and Paul Rand. The Graphic Design Archive, (GDA), is one of the most popular features in the Cary Collection. Its material is shown and studied in a number of classes each semester and is loaned to exhibitions all over the world.

THE CARY COMMUNITY

In choosing the books, manuscripts, art, and realia that appear in this book, Cary curators hope to share our library's highlights, while demonstrating the scope and depth of our collections. When describing a library, it is natural to focus on its collections and the histories of how they were acquired. Perhaps harder to express is the sense of community that is cultivated by libraries like the Cary Collection. In its relatively short time, our library has established itself as much more than a space containing collections. Our space functions as a dynamic site for inspiration, education, and collaboration. More than wood, glass, paper, and skin, the Cary Collection is a vibrant community of friends ranging from students to scholars, artists to graphic designers, typographers to lovers of letterforms.

Nourishing this environment is a policy of liberal access. The Cary Graphic Arts Collection has distinguished itself as a resource that works hard to serve RIT students, faculty, and staff. Each semester, Cary staff teach class sessions for a number of courses across diverse disciplines. Our reading room and exhibition areas host a variety of campus events. International conferences such as Bookbinding 2000 and The Future of Reading Symposium in 2010 have helped introduce our library to the greater scholarly world. But one need not be associated with RIT or another university to take advantage of our library. Even though RIT is a private institution, the public has always been welcome. Our exhibitions and programming are free and open to the public and we are heartened to see the attendance at our events increase year by year. We have also enjoyed watching our user communities grow online through social media.

The Cary Collection is open Monday through Friday and also by appointment. Our contact information is printed below. If you see the warm light of stained-glass calligraphy radiating through the front doors of Cary Collection, you know the library is open and that you are welcome to visit.

Steven K. Galbraith, Curator
Amelia Hugill-Fontanel, Associate Curator
Kari Horowicz, Librarian for the College of Imaging Arts and Sciences

Cary Graphic Arts Collection
Rochester Institute of Technology
90 Lomb Memorial Drive
Rochester, NY 14623
cary.rit.edu
585-475-3961

HIGHLIGHTS OF THE
CARY COLLECTION

CARY'S VISITORS' BOOK
Press of the Woolly Whale. Visitors' Book, 1928–1941. 31 cm.

Melbert B. Cary Jr.'s personal library numbered over 2,300 books on the history and practice of printing, but one book is, in many ways, the heart of the Cary Collection. From 1928 to 1941, guests to Cary's press of the Woolly Whale in New York recorded their names in a visitors' book. The first three people to sign the book were type designer and printer Frederic Goudy, his wife Bertha, and type designer Bruce Rogers. The Goudys and Rogers were followed by a host of noted typographers, artists, printers, and collectors, most of whom are represented in the holdings of the Cary Collection.

Pages from the visitors' book reveal Cary's friendships, as well as his sense of humor. One of the more whimsical entries is a drawing of the Woolly Whale being warned by the gypsy, although the whale doesn't appear to be paying attention. This drawing, at right, is by illustrator Fritz Kredel, whom Cary helped emigrate from Germany in 1938. The drawing below is by Warren Chappell.

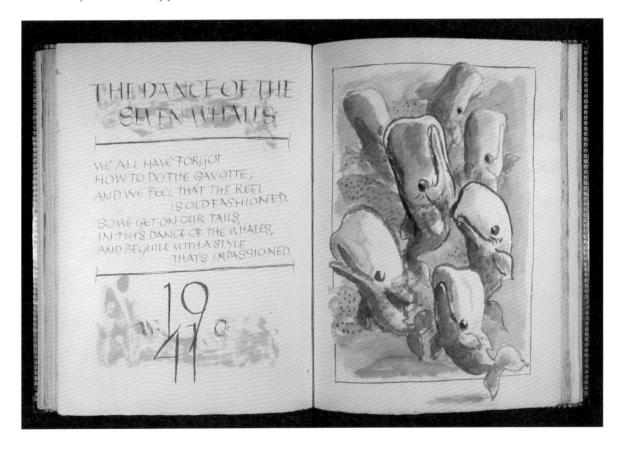

1938

„Listen to the Gypsy's warning…"

THE FRAGMENTS OF LIGHT

Jalaluddin Mohammad Rumi, translation by Zahra Partovi. Glass sculpture by Kelly Driscoll. *Fragments of Light 2*, New York: Vincent FitzGerald & Co., 2003. 26 cm.

Over a 30-year career, publisher Vincent FitzGerald has commissioned artists to re-interpret texts, guiding their creative output into limited-edition bookworks. These *livres d'artistes* are made with myriad techniques including engraving, etching, screen-printing, lithography, and photogravure. Collaboration with artisans is key to synthesizing the final works, which incorporate calligraphy, typography, letterpress printing on custom-made paper, and hand binding. FitzGerald's most recent publications use surprising substrates: carbon steel, glass or Lucite, and even projected light. The combined orchestrated efforts of these books approach the pinnacle of the bookmaking art, and as such, are collected here at the Cary.

The *Fragments of Light* series are five books based on Zahra Partovi's translations of verses of *The Masnavi* by the 13th-century Persian poet Rumi, who wrote about light and all of its physical characteristics to express closeness to God. *Fragments of Light 2*, a stack of glass tablets, may challenge the traditional notion that a book must be a collection of pages bound together. But history tells that books in tablet format are the true antecedents to any tome on paper. Stone, clay, and wax tablets were the most prevalent media for recording and transmitting ancient cultures' written word, long before more supple substrates like papyrus, vellum, or paper were employed. Here, artist Kelly Driscoll expresses the adage "the medium is the message,"[5] as Rumi's Verse 2404 speaks of letting light into the window of the soul. The glass pages become that window, through which "letters rain" via the laser-etched bilingual text. Light plays upon the etching, which even seven-tablets-deep, can be read because of its translucency.

---

5   See note 1, page 1.

THE EARLIEST BOOKS

Cuneiform Tablets, left to right: Lagash, Sumer, c. 2030 BCE;
Old Babylon, c. 1080 BCE; Umma, Sumer, c. 2100 BCE.

Cuneiform tablets are a handheld writing technology that dates back to approximately the 4th millennium BCE. The name comes from the Latin "cuneus" meaning "a wedge," referring to the shape of the impression made when a squared reed is pushed into wet clay. Once the text was inscribed, the tablets were dried in the sun, although not usually fully baked. If not completely dry, the clay could then be rewetted and reused. To prevent tablets from being tampered with, they were sometimes wrapped in clay envelopes. The two smaller tablets shown here are both tablets wrapped in envelopes. This is the most evident with the lighter-colored tablet from Sumer c. 2030 BCE.

Cuneiform tablets are not particularly rare. The Cuneiform Digital Library Initiative estimates that over 500,000 exemplars survive in collections around the world.[6] Yet each is an important piece of history. At the Cary Collection, our three Cuneiform tablets expand our collection's scope to the beginning of writing, and help students living in a modern tablet culture understand that the technology of handheld, re-writable tablets is actually four thousand years old.

---

6   "About CDLI," Cuneiform Digital Library Initiative, http://cdli.ucla.edu/?q=about.

MOVEABLE PRINTING TYPE

Printing Type, Korea, c. 1400. 14 × 11 mm (peace), 12 × 9 mm (air).

In 1040 CE in China, Bì Shēng (990–1051) made the first moveable printing type using clay. A century later, Chinese printers were working with type made from wood. By the early 13th century, bronze moveable type was in limited use in Korea and China. The two pieces of metal type shown here are likely examples of Korean moveable type from the early 15th century. These characters representing "air" and "peace" predate Gutenberg's invention of type in the West by 50 years. They rest along side examples of Goudy Text type cast in the 20th century.

Metal printing type produced in Asia differed from those later produced in Europe in that the characters were made of bronze cast in sand. In Europe, type was made of an alloy of lead, tin, and antimony, and was cast using a system of metal matrices (page 60) and a hand mold (shown below). The methods of printing differed, too. In Asia, paper was placed atop the inked type and rubbed with a burnisher to create the impression. In Europe, printers used printing presses.

THE GUTENBERG BIBLE

Biblia Latina. [Leaf 308]. Mainz: Printer of the 42-line Bible (Johann Gutenberg & Peter Schöffer) between 1454 and 1455, not after August 1456.

Although the art of printing with moveable type was invented in China, it was popularized in Europe by Johann Gutenberg (c. 1397–1468) who in the 1450s, independently developed a system for printing using moveable metal type and a printing press. Gutenberg's invention quickly spread from his hometown of Mainz, Germany to the rest of world. His first book was an edition of the Latin or Vulgate translation of the Bible produced by St. Jerome (d. 419 or 420) in the 4th century.

Forty-nine copies of the Gutenberg Bible survive, twenty-one of which are complete.[7] The Cary Collection has the good fortune of owning two leaves from the Gutenberg Bible: one leaf from the Book of Jeremiah and another pictured here from the Book of Psalms. A close look at the page reveals that the first printed books were actually hybrid documents that contained manuscript and printed elements. For example, the large blue initial letter Q and the red initial M beneath it were supplied in manuscript, that is, by hand and not printed. Showing further influences of manuscript, Gutenberg created a variety of forms for each letter, both to accommodate the marks needed for the contractions used in Latin manuscripts, and also to make the type look more natural, imitating human writing.

---

7   For an excellent introduction to the Gutenberg Bible see: http://www.hrc.utexas.edu/exhibitions/permanent/gutenbergbible/.

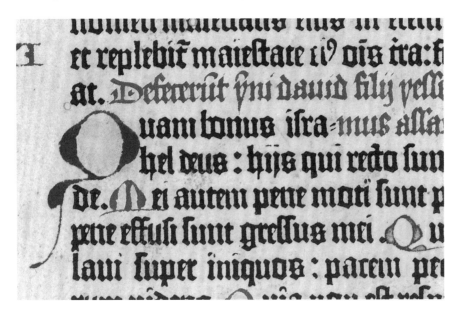

usqz in altissima que fecisti magnalia : deus quis similis sit tibi ? Quantas ostendisti michi tribulationes multas et malas : et conuersus viuificasti me : et de abissis terre iterum reduxisti me. Multiplicasti magnificentiam tuam : et conuersus consolatus es me. Nam et ego confitebor tibi in vasis psalmi veritatem tuam deus : psallam tibi in cythara sanctus israhel. Exultabunt labia mea cum cantauero tibi et aia mea quam redemisti. Sed et lingua mea tota die meditabit iusticiam tuam : cum confusi et reueriti fuerit qui querunt mala michi. In salomone LXXI

Deus iudicium tuum regi da : et iusticiam tuam filio regis. Iudicare populum tuum in iusticia : et pauperes tuos in iudicio. Suscipiant montes pacem populo : et colles iusticiam. Iudicabit pauperes populi et saluos faciet filios pauperum : et humiliabit calumniatorem. Et permanebit cum sole et ante lunam : in generatione et generatione. Descendet sicut pluuia in vellus : et sicut stillicidia stillantia super terram. Orietur in diebus eius iusticia et abundantia pacis : donec auferatur luna. Et dominabitur a mari usqz ad mare : et a flumine usqz ad terminos orbis terrarum. Coram illo procident ethiopes : et inimici eius terram lingent. Reges tharsis et insule munera offerent : reges arabum et saba dona adducent. Et adorabunt eum omnes reges : omnes gentes seruient ei. Quia liberabit pauperem a potente : et pauperem cui non erat adiutor. arcet pauperi et inopi : et animas pauperum saluas faciet. Ex usuris et iniquitate redimet animas eorum :

et honorabile nomen eorum coram illo. Et viuet et dabitur ei de auro arabie : et adorabunt de ipso semper : tota die benedicent ei. Erit firmamentum in terra in summis montium : superextolletur super libanum fructus eius : et florebunt de ciuitate sicut fenum terre. Sit nomen eius benedictum in secula : ante solem permanet nomen eius. Et benedicentur in ipso omnes tribus terre : omnes gentes magnificabunt eum. Benedictus dominus deus israhel : qui facit mirabilia solus. Et benedictum nomen maiestatis eius in eternum : et replebit maiestate eius omnis terra : fiat fiat. Defecerunt hymni dauid filij yesse. Psalmus asaph. LXXII

Quam bonus israhel deus : hiis qui recto sunt corde. Mei autem pene moti sunt pedes : pene effusi sunt gressus mei. Quia zelaui super iniquos : pacem peccatorum videns. Quia non est respectus morti eorum : et firmamentum in plaga eorum. In labore hominum non sunt : et cum hominibus non flagellabuntur. Ideo tenuit eos superbia : operti sunt iniquitate et impietate sua. Prodijt quasi ex adipe iniquitas eorum : transierunt in affectum cordis. Cogitauerunt et locuti sunt nequiciam : iniquitatem in excelso locuti sunt. Posuerunt in celum os suum : et lingua eorum transiuit in terra. Ideo conuertetur populus meus hic : et dies pleni inuenientur in eis. Et dixerunt quomodo scit deus : et si est scientia in excelso ? Ecce ipsi peccatores et abundantes in seculo : obtinuerunt diuitias. Et dixi ergo sine causa iustificaui cor meum : et laui inter innocentes manus meas. Et fui flagellatus tota die :

PRINTING MEDALS

Pierre I, King of Cyprus, c. 14th century. Silver, 26 mm.

Gutenberg & Fust. Leipzig, 1740. Medalist: Jean Dassier (1676–1763). Silver, 42 mm.

Louis Braille. France, 1975. Gilded bronze, 68 mm.

Fourth Centenary of Printing in Mexico. Mexico, 1939. Gilded bronze, 40 mm.

Gutenberg's standing in the history of printing is reflected in the Printing Medal Collection of printer Erich Wronker. Acquired by Cary in 2002, this distinctive collection consists of over 800 medals and assorted artifacts from twenty-seven different countries. They commemorate famous inventors, places, events, and, of course, printers. It comes as no surprise that Johann Gutenberg is the most frequently depicted figure in the Wronker Collection. For example, a silver medal issued in Germany in 1740 positions Gutenberg facing his business partner Johann Fust.

Erich Wronker's first acquisition was a 14th-century crusader coin of Pierre de Lusignan, or Peter I of Cyprus (1328–1369). As his wife Lili Cassel-Wronker has written, "During World War II, Erich was sent to Cyprus with the British 8th Army. There, at Othello's castle, he found crusader coins."[8] Surveying the assortment of medals he acquired over his lifetime is a study in the history of printing and of written communication. A medal struck in Mexico in 1939, for example, commemorates the 500th anniversary of the founding of a printing press by Juan Pablos (Giovanni Paoli, d. 1561) in Mexico City, the first in North America. Another produced in France in 1975 celebrates the life of Louis Braille (1806–1852), who invented the system of writing for the blind that takes his name. The back of the coin reads "et la lumière fut" (Genesis 1:3, "And there was light") in French and in braille.

8   Lili Wronker, "Selections from the Printing Medal Collections of Erich Wronker," (handwritten manuscript, 2002).

15TH-CENTURY BOOK ILLUSTRATION
Printing-block (woodcut). Jesus and the Apostles. c. 1500. 192 × 129 cm.

The earliest illustrations used in printed books were produced using woodcut blocks, a technology that predated printing with moveable type by centuries. In this process, an artist carves an illustration or text in relief (reverse) into a block of wood and usually parallel to the long grain. The block's thickness is approximately "type-high," or the same height as the metal moveable type, thus the woodcut illustration and the type would be inked and printed at the same time.

The Cary Collection preserves an example of a woodcut that appears to date back to the late 15th or early 16th century, and is possibly of German origin. The illustration depicts Christ teaching his apostles—perhaps the Parable of the Workers in the Vineyard. The book or books in which this illustration might have appeared have yet to be identified. Woodcuts from this period were rarely designed for just one book, but would be reused when the subject matter suited them. The wear shown on this block is less from printing than from insects, especially bookworms, for which wood is especially tasty. They are responsible for the numerous tiny holes found on the block.

PENNYROYAL CAXTON BIBLE

The Holy Bible: Containing All the Books of the Old and New Testaments.
North Hatfield, Mass.: Pennyroyal Caxton Press, 1999.
Cary's copy is 79 of the 400 printed.

In the 18th century, the art of carving illustrations into wood blocks evolved. Rather than using a knife to carve into the long grain of wood, artists began using a burin to engrave fine lines into the end grain of the wood. The end grain is exposed when the wood is cut at a 90° angle, resulting in a hard surface that can hold delicate lines similar to those engraved into metal surfaces, such as copper. One of the modern masters of the art is Barry Moser (b. 1940), whose masterpiece is the Pennyroyal Caxton Bible.

The Pennyroyal Caxton Bible has crowned over four centuries of fine editions of the Bible, from Gutenberg's *Biblia Sacra* c. 1455 to Bradbury Thompson's *Washburn College Bible* in 1979. It is the first illustrated Bible in a century with images made by a single artist, and the first fine press Bible of its scale that blends traditional letterpress printing with modern digital typesetting.

"Ever since I set my first line of type I have dreamt of doing a Bible," explains Moser. "It is in fact the Everest for a typographer or an illustrator."[9] Moser carved 230 original relief engravings, illustrating each Bible chapter from the King James Version translation. His images are dramatic and moving as they are based on compositions with live models, imparting a contemporary freshness to the ancient stories. These are printed on a Zerkall paper, specially commissioned for the project. The plates enhance the text that is set in Matthew Carter's elegant Galliard and Mantinia typefaces, with initial lettering designed by John Benson. Printing for the two-volume folio edition was completed over two years—a labor of great magnitude, even when using the conveniences of computer-based design and plastic relief plates, instead of handset metal type. Each volume is bound in vellum with gold hand tooling.

Through the history of the printed word in the Western world, the Bible stands out as the most reproduced text, with Cary Collection holdings evenly documenting some of its most important editions. The Pennyroyal Caxton joined the suite of landmark Biblical interpretations here, as a gift from RIT's Vice President Emeritus, Alfred L. Davis.

---

9   *A Thief Among the Angels: A Documentary Film about the Making of the Pennyroyal Caxton Bible.* New York and London: The Kessler Company, c. 1998.

JONAH

AND THE SEA CEASED RAGING

THE FIRST BOOK OF MOSES CALLED GENESIS

GOD

CREATED THE HEAVEN AND THE EARTH. AND THE EARTH WAS WITHOUT FORM, AND VOID; AND DARKNESS WAS UPON THE FACE OF THE DEEP. AND THE SPIRIT OF GOD MOVED UPON THE FACE OF THE WATERS. AND GOD SAID, LET THERE BE LIGHT: AND THERE WAS LIGHT. AND GOD SAW THE LIGHT, THAT IT WAS GOOD: AND GOD DIVIDED THE LIGHT FROM THE DARKNESS. AND GOD CALLED THE LIGHT DAY, AND THE DARKNESS HE CALLED NIGHT. AND THE EVENING AND THE MORNING WERE THE FIRST DAY. AND GOD SAID, LET THERE BE A FIRMAMENT IN THE MIDST OF THE WATERS, AND LET IT DIVIDE THE WATERS FROM THE WATERS. ... made the firmament, and divided the ... under the firmament from ... the firmament: ...

lights; the greater light to rule the day, and the lesser light to rule the night: he made the stars also. And God set them in the firmament of the heaven to give light upon the earth, And to rule over the day and over the night, and to divide ... the darkness: and God saw that ... evening and the morning ... said, Let the ... crea-

TWO EDITIONS OF HORACE

Horace. *Horativs*. Venetiis: Apvd Aldvm Romanvm, Mense Maio, 1501.

Horace. *Quinti Horatii Flacci Opera*. Londini: Aeneis tabulis Incidit Iohannes Pine, 1733–1737.

The works of the Roman poet Quintus Horatius Flaccus (65–8 BCE), more commonly known as Horace, have been the subject of two landmarks in the history of printing. In 1501, Venetian printer Aldus Manutius (1449 or 50–1515) initiated a series of pocket-sized octavo editions of classical authors. The first two books in this series were an edition of the works of the Roman poet Virgil, printed in April 1501, followed a month later with an edition of the works of Horace. Not only did these books help popularize portable octavo books, they were also the first two books to use Aldus's newly cast italic typeface. Today we think of italic as a companion to a roman face, but Aldus' italic was based on an early 15th-century Italian Humanist script. Decades later Claude Garamond would design an italic typeface as "a consciously formed complement to the roman."[10]

More than two centuries after Aldus's innovations, the works of Horace played a part in another printing milestone. In 1733, John Pine (1690–1756) produced an edition of the works of Horace in which the text was printed not with moveable type, but rather with the entire text engraved into copper plates. There must have been great interest in Pine's bibliographic experiment, for the printed list of subscribers is as long as it is illustrious. Among those who purchased their books in advance were the King of England, the Prince of Wales, and a variety of other English nobility, as well as the King of Portugal, the King of France, and the King and Queen of Spain.

Whereas Aldus's innovations had a long-lasting impact on the art of printing, Pine's experiment never become commonplace. Pine's engraved volumes are certainly elegant, but the process made it very difficult to correct mistakes. Printing complete books with copper plates was ultimately not a viable method of printing.

---

10   Alexander S. Lawson, *Printing Types: An Introduction* (Boston: Beacon Press, 1990), 61.

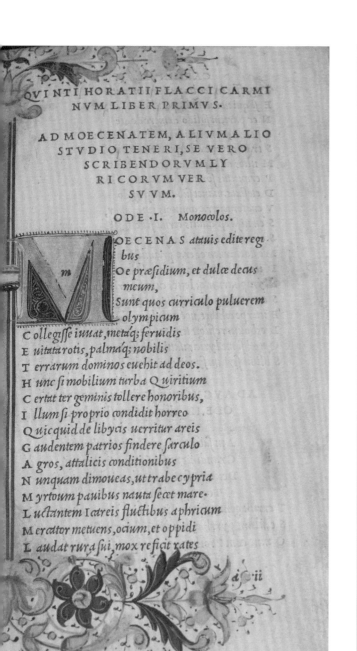

QVINTI HORATII FLACCI CARMI
NVM LIBER PRIMVS.

AD MOECENATEM, ALIVM ALIO
STVDIO TENERI, SE VERO
SCRIBENDORVM LY
RICORVM VER
SVVM.

ODE ·I· *Monocolos.*

M OECENAS *atauis edite regi
bus,
Oe præsidium, et dulcæ decus
meum,
Sunt quos curriculo puluerem
olympicum*

C *ollegisse iuuat, metaq; feruidis*
E *uitata rotis, palmaq; nobilis*
T *errarum dominos euehit ad deos.*
H *unc si mobilium turba Quiritium*
C *ertat ter geminis tollere honoribus,*
I *llum si proprio condidit horreo*
Q *uicquid de libycis uerritur areis*
G *audentem patrios findere sarculo*
A *gros, attalicis conditionibus*
N *unquam dimoueas, ut trabe cypria*
M *yrtoum pauibus nauta secet mare.*
L *uctantem Icareis fluctibus aphricum*
M *ercator metuens, ocium, et oppidi*
L *audat rura sui, mox reficit rates*

a ii

QVINTI
HORATII FLACCI
CARMINVM
LIBER I.

ODE I.
AD MAECENATEM.

 M AECENAS atavis edite regibus,
O et praesidium et dulce decus meum,
Sunt quos curriculo pulverem Olym-
picum

Collegisse juvat; metaque fervidis
Evitata rotis, palmaque nobilis   5
Terrarum dominos evehit ad Deos.
Hunc, si mobilium turba Quiritium
Certat tergeminis tollere honoribus;
Illum, si proprio condidit horreo
Quidquid de Libycis verritur areis,   10

A

"THE ART OF THE BOOK"

Masao Yamamoto. *Yamamoto Masao.* South Dennis, Mass.: 21st Editions, 2010–2011. Deluxe Edition. Text and a poem by John Wood. Photographs by Masao Yamamoto. Edition: 42. Two volumes hand-bound in silk. 12 bound platinum prints and 3 loose silver gelatin prints. 31.75 cm.

21st Editions is a modern press whose works endeavor to exhibit the finest qualities of book production, a goal expressed in their motto, "The Art of the Book." Best known perhaps for fine art photography paired with literature and poetry, their books also merge the arts of letterpress printing, papermaking, and bookbinding, making their books a natural fit for the Cary Collection. Thirty-four 21st Editions titles are held within the Cary Collection and titles are carefully selected yearly.

Interacting with their Deluxe Edition of the photography book *Yamamoto Masao* in particular, provides the full experience of the book as art. Yamamoto (b. 1957), originally trained as a painter, has been a fine art photographer since 1975. His finished photographs are typically small, and are toned and stained to create an aged appearance that evokes the past.

Yamamoto has written, "I hope a good ki (circulating life energy in all things) cleanses people's minds while it circulates as breath. And as an artist, I believe art, such as drawings and photographs, are here to help that flow."[11] This natural circulation of ki is activated through the calm and beauty of his photographs, while their presentation by the artists of 21st Editions stimulates the senses.

Two silk-bound portfolios rest carefully in a cedar box, quickening the reader's senses of touch and smell. The cedar box is one of the artifacts in the Cary Collection that offers an aromatic experience. Yamamoto's platinum and silver gelatin prints present natural subjects such as landscapes, nudes, and insects in way that makes them seem ancient and timeless. As Dan Leers has written "Yamamoto often engages with nature by collecting specimens. He ensnares birds and insects with his camera, displaying them as if they were in a natural history museum diorama or trapped in a piece of amber jewellery."[12] Viewing this book within the quiet of the Cary reading room completes the experience.

---

11   Masao Yamamoto, *Where We Met* (Tielt, Belgium: Lannoo Books, 2011), 13.
12   Ibid, 8.

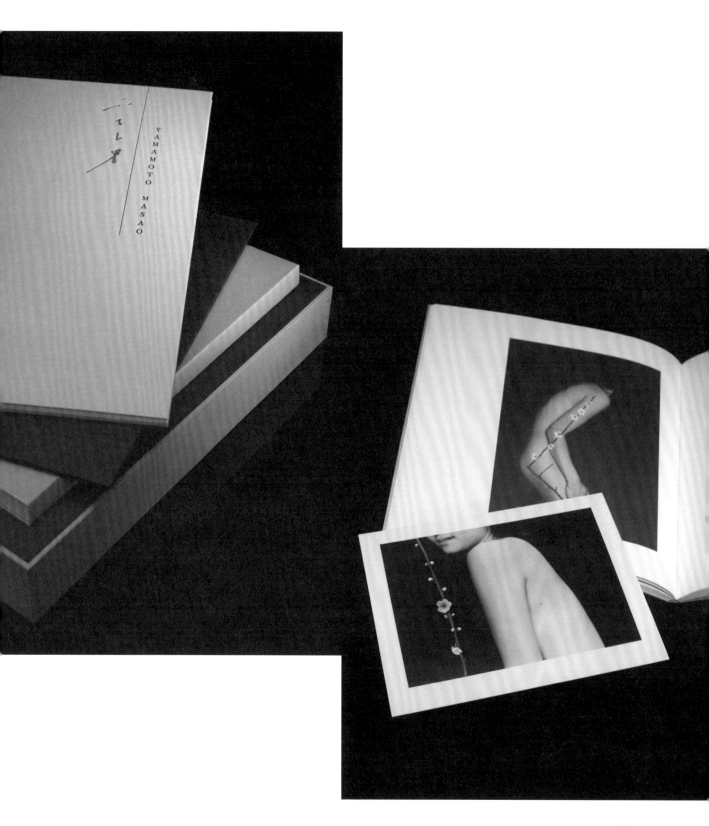

THE FIRST NEWSPAPER

Rodericus Zamorensis. *Epistola de expugnatione Nigropontis*.
Cologne: Ulrich Zel, circa 1470–71.

In 1982, the Cary Collection experienced a major transformational moment with the acquisition of *The New York Times* Museum of the Recorded Word. Many of the artifacts in the museum's collection relate to the history of printed news, such as a pamphlet printed in 1470–71 titled *Epistola de expugnatione Nigropontis* or "A letter on the siege of Negroponte." The text is a contemporary account of the Turkish siege of Negroponte (Euboea), which had been under the rule of the Venetian Empire. Because this might have been the first time contemporary news was printed, some scholars view this pamphlet as possibly being the first example of what came to be known centuries later as a newspaper.

Scholars of the history of the book are often interested in how owners of books interacted with them. One way to study this is by examining handwritten annotations and markings in books. The Cary Collection copy of *Epistola de expugnatione Nigropontis* has several decorative examples of manuscript annotation inscribed by an early reader. Several passages are marked with brackets that look almost like comical human faces. Other lines of texts are literally pointed to by elegant manicules, or drawings of pointing hands. Manicules are commonly found in early books and perform the function that highlighting and underlining do for modern readers.

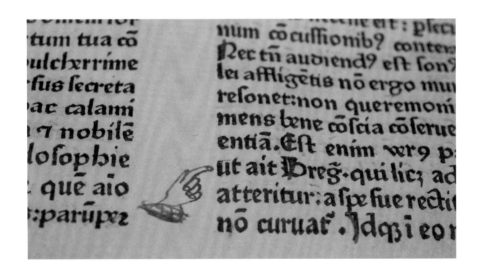

pmitter:nisi ex illis bona et no
bis pfitura elicer. Idco igitur
hac nos acerba clade affligere
pmittit:ut caucō res atcz feruen
cōtes n nos reddat cōtra hostes
fidei. Sepx enim ut sacri interp
tes aiunt:de? flagellari ꝗ oteri
fideles suos pmittit:ut er ipso
vulnere a ruina erudiantur et
fortius rsurgant ad pfligādos
hostes spuales ꝙ cōpares qui
nos afflixerūt. Ruo fit ut eodē
Augustino teste:vitam morta
liū ipa diuina puidētia varijs
psecucōibus exercet:pzobatā
ꝗ meliora transfert ꝗ ꝗ bonos
vsus fideliū vrtit. Adde ꝗ ut
aiunt afflictō dat intellectū:et
plerūꝗ fideles quos intestina
diuisio ad ruinā pdunt:ipse
dolor illate cladis atcz ad coē
hoste paucos vnanimes efficit.
Vt enim ait philosoph?timor
cois in inmicos ꝗ dissidentes concj
liat. Erit igitur ut pie speramus
hec calamitas signū in bonū:ꝙ
cōspecta cūcti fideles eo archus
cōtra crucis xpi hostes insurgēt
ut multitudo credebitum fit cor
nu ꝗ anima vna:Et tāto iā for
tius sese in hostes vniant quāto
piculosius diuisi sucumbunt:si
cut scriptum est. Effusa est con
tenco inter principes ꝗ errare e
os fecit in via. Sic enim scrip
tura cōmemorat quoniam rex
Arad populū Israhel diuisum ꝗ

dissidētē grauiter afflixit. Isi
vero se vnientes ac vro se obli
gantes hoste suparūt:ꝗ ciuita
tes pditas recuprarūt:sic ob dis
sidiū inter domum Saulis et
domū dauid filistei vtrūcz per
cusserūt:si tandem ex ea pcussi
one animos virescz reassumen
tes ꝗ quasi vir vnus sedenti ho
stes a finib? Israhel puleriūt:hic
refert. Orosius Sapioné cōtu
eum quēdam interrogasse cur
numāta piꝗ mūcta pt9 vro
euersa foret. At ille concordia
inquit Numātū victoriā pe
pit:discordia excidiū. Deniꝗ
illud vrū est:ꝙ nemine fallit
qui suo incōmutabili verbo ec
clesiā suā de camino tribulacōnū
saluare policitus est. Cum scri
ptū sit:dispoluit librare eā de
medio ꝗ inimicor ei9. Adeo ei sibi
dilecā est ut se ea ꝗ ꝗ apha ai dixerū
Ruid potui facere ꝗ vinee mee ꝗ
nō feci:ꝙ igitur cō in nos ex
arset i breui ira ci9. Ruis scit si
ouertetur ꝗ ignoset:ꝗ reliquet
post se benedictōnē:Quare cō
fidetissime Rex a ꝗpha dicebat
Cum iratus fueris misericordie
recordaberis.Percutit sepe fide
suos diuina prouidentia et
ꝗ infideles cruciat.Sed tandē
osolacōes ipsis tribuit tbulatis
dicente ꝗpha.O quātas osten
disti nob tribulacōes multas
ꝗ magnas.Sz illico sequitur.

Et ouersus viuificasti me:ꝗ ꝗso
latus es me.Nō nūꝗ vero eos
dem infideles seuiter supra lo
ganimitas tollerat:ut extrema
iudicij seueitas puniat.sic sci
ptū e.Sup tribulātes eos ꝗ int
tetet manū suā.Nō ergo oturbe
mur ex hac pfidi hostis illata
clade.potes ei ꝗ ꝗ irat9 eā intu
lit placat9 ꝗ ecie pfcm ouerte
re.Deo enim sanguis suor
suor9 efusus e:si intrabit i ꝗspe
ctu ei9 gemit9 opeditor:ipse
est ꝗ extrema luctu ouertit pla
billi:ꝗ teste ꝗpha ouerit plā
ctum nrm in gaudiū.Scriptū
e ei qui pausit ꝗ dispsie Israhel
ipse ogregabit ꝗ librabit eū de
manu potēonis:ꝗ demꝗ cō
uertā luctū eor ꝗ leticiā ꝗ ꝗso
lab9 eos ꝗ leticabit a dolore
suo.Rā a apud Ezechiele i ꝗpo
recēti vulnere cōsolacō ꝗ poli
cetur pso suo.Postꝗ iꝗt cō
pleuero furore meu ꝗescere fa
ciam indignacōnē meā ꝗ cōso
lab9 eos a fsiet ꝗ ego dns.
Fallere ꝙd veritas nō pot ꝗ ꝗ
sapiente hostis fidei excidiū cō
mnatur.homo iꝗt apostata
subito cōteretur:ꝗ stati dū nō
speratur vniet cōtricō ei9.spe
rem9 igitur in eū ꝗ eciā nobis
adiutoꝗ ꝗ opoztunitatib9 a in
tribulacōne:a potēcia inimico
rū facile dissoluet:aut in nrm de
dicōnem ouertz.sicut scriptū

est.In spū vhementi cōterz na
ues tarssis.idest dissipātis.In
pzimo nēpe est ut nos cōsole
tur.non enim vsꝗ in fine irasci
tur de?:quippe ipsa scriptuā te
ste statim post vicōne pstat be
neficiū.Idcꝗ inoubie experi
mur:si a sꝗx dni pfidij nō exci
derim9:si pacienter easdē pseu
cōnes in nostris fratribus ptu
lerim9:ꝗs ipei ꝗpia vdū in hac
mortli aggerit vita ꝗ nobis ꝗ
psius e.Sic eni nos admoni
eis vlaisceis oes ad inuecones
eoꝗ.Sic a ad beatū Job pt9
seua flagella amic9 Eliphas
dicebat:btius homo qui corri
pitur a dno a inuemet eū si in
tribulacōne clamauerit.ipse e
clemētissim9 de? ꝗ Amos pro
plxtā ait:tātum vos cogno
ui ex oib? cognacōbz.Idcir
co visitatoꝗ vos sup oes iniꝗta
tes vris.Aue verba Bernar
dus exponēs iꝗt:vult facere se
cognosciuertzcōco:ꝗ nri obli
tus erat tolleracō.Porro agit
nobiscū pfissim9 deus ut pater
indulgētissim9.ꝗ filios caiores

PRINTER TO THE AMERICAN REVOLUTION

Massachusetts Spy. Vol. 5, no. 227 (June 28, 1775).
Thomas Almanacs. 1780–1826.

"Americans! Liberty or Death! Join or Die!" announces the banner of
The Massachusetts Spy. Published by printer Isaiah Thomas (1749–1831)
beginning in 1770, this radical newspaper actively promoted the
American Revolution with articles describing the injustices against the
colonies and news from the battlefield. Thomas's delivery riders even
served double-duty as intelligence couriers for the patriots.

After the Revolution, Isaiah Thomas issued the kinds of publications
that were in demand in his time: bibles, primers, and almanacs. It has been
said that, "The Bible took care of the hereafter, but the almanac took care of
the here."[13] Thomas published his almanacs almost yearly from 1775 until
1803. Examples held in the Cary Collection are small pamphlets, about
the size of a paperback. Even the poorest readers would have been able to
afford these inexpensive booklets. Thomas is said to have to reprinted each
edition two or three times to keep up with demand.

---

13   Marion Barber Stowell, *Early American Almanacs* (NY: Burt Franklin, 1977), viii.

TEACHING CHILDREN TO READ
Hornbook. England, c. 1600. 23.8 × 12.2 cm.

Named for the thin layer of animal horn that protected the printed text, hornbooks were tools used to teach children to read from the 15th through the early 18th century in England and America.[14] The instructional text, which usually consisted of the alphabet in upper and lower case and the "Our Father" prayer, was attached to a wooden or metal paddle that would be held in front of a child who would practice reading.

The Cary Collection owns an extraordinary example of a hornbook dating to England c. 1600, as evidenced by the brass bosses decorating the calfskin binding. Each boss is ornamented with the Tudor rose, an ornament popular in England even after the death of Queen Elizabeth I in 1603 ended the Tudor reign.

---

14   Andrew White Tuer, *History of the Horn-book* (Amsterdam: S. Emmering, 1971), 5–9.

Aabcdefghi
klmnopqrs
stvuwxyz.
abcdefghiklmnop
qrstuwxyz

Our Father, which art in heaven,

(text illegible)

...wine us from
Power, and glorie, for ever, Amen.

BOOKBINDER'S INDENTURE

Indenture of Edward Wheatley, apprenticed to Thomas Richardson & Son
Bookbinders of Derby. Derby, England: s.n., 1842.
Signed on April 19, 1842. Parchment. 35.5 × 25.0 cm.

Found in the Cary Collection's Bernard C. Middleton Collection of Books
on the History and Practice of Bookbinding is this indenture spelling out
the conditions of Edward Wheatley's apprenticeship to the bookbinders
Thomas Richardson & Son. With the consent of his father William Wheatley, Edward signed on for a seven-year apprenticeship, committing to
work six days a week ("Sunday alone excepted") from "six o'clock in the
morning until 8 o'clock in the evening." Part of the agreement is to not
haunt "Tavern, Inns, or Alehouses" or play "Cards, Dice Tables, or any
other unlawful Games."

Although "indenture" has evolved into a general term for a deed or
contract, it originally referenced the actual document's indented edges.
A legal document was written twice on one piece of parchment (animal
skin) and then cut into two halves, one for each party. To prove that the
document was genuine, when reunited, the indented edges of the two
halves should be a perfect match. In this case, Edward Wheatley and
Thomas Richardson would each have a signed copy of the indenture.
Artifacts like this are often quite ephemeral, but perhaps the other half
of this document still survives.

This Indenture witnesseth, That Edward Wheatley, by and with the

consent of his Father William Wheatley, Frameworkknitter of the parish of St All mundes in the Borough of Derby

doth put h___ self APPRENTICE to Thomas Richardson & Son of Derby Bookbinders

to learn h___ ___ and their ___ and with ___ them after the manner of an Apprentice, to serve from the day of the date of these presents

unto the full End and Term of Seven Years, from thence next following, to be fully complete and ended; during which Term the said Apprentice h__ said Masters faithfully shall serve, their Secrets keep, their lawful Commands every-where gladly do, he shall do no Damage to h is said Masters nor see it done by others, but to h is power shall let or forthwith give warning to h is said Masters of the same; he shall not waste the goods of h is said Masters nor give or lend them unlawfully to any; he shall neither buy nor sell without h is said M asters leave; Taverns, Inns, or Alehouses, he shall not haunt; at Cards, Dice Tables, or any other unlawful Games he shall not play; Matrimony he shall not contract: nor from the service of h is said Masters Day or Night absent himself; but in all Things, as a faithful Apprentice he shall behave himself towards h is said Masters and all their Family, during the said Term.—AND the said Thomas Richardson & Son for themselves their Heirs Executors and Administrators and for every of these both promise and agree to and with the said William Wheatley his Heirs and assigns that they the said Thomas Richardson &c. for and in consideration of the Sum of services of the said Apprentice to ___ well and faithfully to h___ in hand well and truly paid by performed their the Receipt whereof is hereby acknowledged, the said Apprentice in the Art of a Bookbinder which he now useth, shall and will teach and instruct, or cause to be taught and instructed, in the best way and manner that ___ ___; and shall find unto the said Apprentice sufficient Meat, Drink, in lieu of Meat, Drink, Lodging, and all other Necessaries during the said Term the weekly wages following, that is to say the sum of Two Shillings and Sixpence per week for the first year, three shillings per week for the second year, four shillings per week for the third year, five shillings per week for the fourth year, five shillings and sixpence per week for the fifth year, six shillings per week for the sixth year, and seven shillings per week for the seventh and last year of the said Term. The time of attendance for each and every day of the afore said Term of Seven years (Sundays alone excepted) to be from Six o'clock in the morning until eight o'clock in the evening. The said wages to cease and determine during the absence from sickness or any other cause and leave of the said apprentice from the service of his said Masters without the consent or direction of his said Masters in writing

AND for the true Performance of all and every the said Covenants and Agreements, each of the said Parties bindeth him self unto the other firmly by these Presents.—IN WITNESS whereof, the Parties abovesaid to these Indentures have hereunto interchangeably set their Hands and Seals the Nineteenth Day of April in the Sixth Year of the Reign of our Sovereign Lady Victoria, by the Grace of God, of the United Kingdom of Great Britain and Ireland, Queen, Defender of the Faith, and in the Year of our LORD One Thousand Eight Hundred and Forty two.

Sealed and delivered (being first duly stamped) in the presence of } Thomas Popple

Edward Wheatley

William Wheatley

Thomas Richardson & Son

41

EDWARDS OF HALIFAX

John Watson. *The History and Antiquities of the Parish of Halifax, in Yorkshire*.
London: T. Lowndes, 1775.

The Middleton Collection of Books on the History and Practice of Bookbinding also features specimens of fine and historical bookbindings. One such example is from the Edwards of Halifax bindery, which popularized several bookbinding styles in the mid 18th and early 19th centuries. Shown here is a copy of *The History and Antiquities of the Parish of Halifax* with an Etruscan calf binding. The term Etruscan comes from the use of classical ornamentation like the palmettes that make up the dark border within the outer gold-tooled border. The center panel is an example of tree calf — calfskin decorated by staining it with acid so that the surface of the skin looks like wood grain.

Another decorative element sometimes found on Edwards of Halifax bindings is hidden fore-edge painting. To achieve this effect, a painting is applied to the fore-edge (or long edge opposite the spine) of a book with gilt edges while the book is fanned open in a book clamp. When the book is closed, the painting disappears behind the layer of gold. When the book is fanned, the painting reappears. The Cary Collection's copy of *The History and Antiquities of the Parish of Halifax* features a fore-edge painting of "the South East View of the Town of Halifax" based on an engraved illustration that appears in the book.

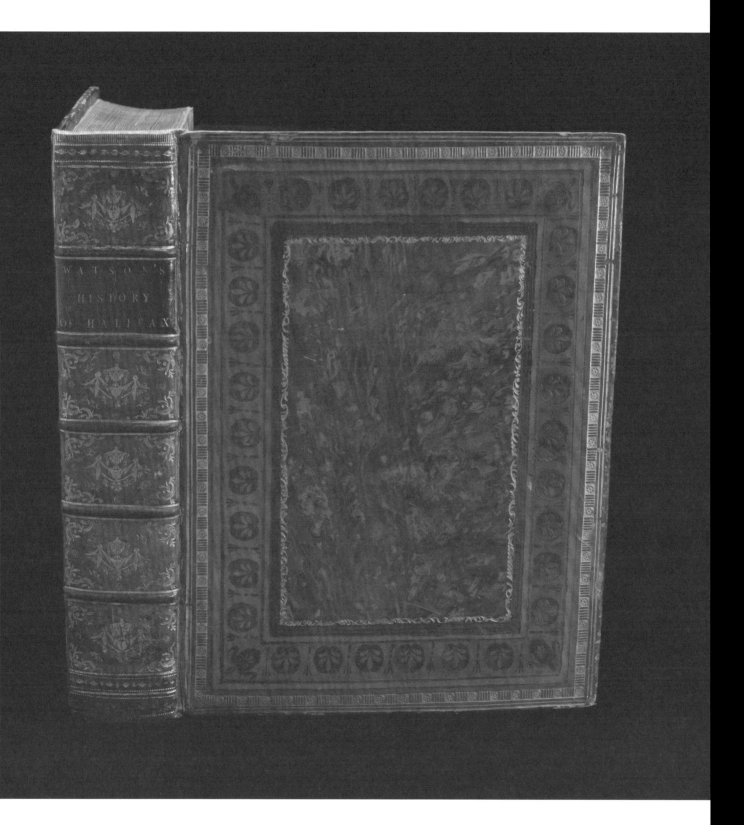

BRODOVITCH

Portfolio: A Magazine for the Graphic Arts, Volume 1, number 1, Winter 1950. Editors: George S. Rosenthal, Frank Zachary. Art Editor: Alexey Brodovitch. Zebra Press, 1950. 33 × 25.5 cm.

Portfolio: A Magazine for the Graphic Arts (1950–1951) was an innovative experiment in editorial design. Famed art director Alexey Brodovitch collaborated with fellow art director Frank Zachary and publisher/printer George Rosenthal to challenge the limits of an editorial publication. Without the constraints of advertisers, they created an extraordinary publication which combined unique inserts, unusual substrates, extended fold-outs with interesting articles looking at influential artists and designers, both current and historical, and incorporated articles about contemporary culture.

The first issue is bookended with articles devoted to Giambattista Bodoni, commencing with a historical article on Bodoni's evolution as a type designer and concluding with an article on how contemporary designers of the 1950s used Bodoni's typeface in their designs. Designers highlighted include Bradbury Thompson, Paul Rand, Alexander Lieberman, and Alvin Lustig.

The page spread seen here features elegant Arabic numerals reproduced from Bodoni's *Manuale Tipografico*, the insert of facsimile specimen pages printed on handmade paper from the Cartier Miliani, the historic paper mill in Fabriano, Italy which supplied Bodoni with similar paper, and a portrait of Bodoni.

Some design historians state that Brodovitch used Bodoni as his typeface of choice while others attribute it to Didot. Still others write that it is true Didone, a merger of the two faces.[15] However, there is no doubt that the elegant modern face of Bodoni is an inspiration and Michel Brodovitch, Alexey Brodovitch's cousin, believes that Brodovitch used his own copy of the *Manuale Tipografico* for the reproductions in this first issue.[16] *Portfolio* is set entirely in a modern Bodoni interpretation—Lanston Monotype Bodoni Book 875.

Portfolio, frequently cited as one of the key graphic design magazines of the 20th century, is part of the vast journal holdings within the Cary Collection, which is rich in publications dealing with the graphic arts. In addition, *Portfolio* is part of the Alexey Brodovitch Collection which in recent years is one of the most popular archives with researchers and museum curators visiting from all over the world to examine it.

---

15 Paul Shaw and Stephen Coles, "Ruder's Univers, Weingart's Akzidenz, Vignelli's Haas, Brodovitch's Didone," *Print*, vol. 65, issue 5, (October 2011), 39.

16 Kerry William Purcell, *Alexey Brodovitch* (New York: Phaidon, 2002), 205, 266.

BODONI

Giambattista Bodoni. *Manuale Tipografico del Cavaliere Giambattista Bodoni*. Parma: Presso la Vedova, 1818.

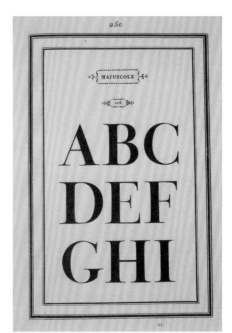

Type specimens are promotional materials like books, pamphlets, and now websites, which are published by printers and type founders to show their typefaces. This genre of catalog that dates to the 15th century is sometimes mundane in its simplicity, or it can be inventive and luxurious. Examples of type specimens are found in almost every book and archival collection at the Cary, making up a prominent collecting focus in the library. Featured here among the thousands of such specimens, is the one that has exerted such influence even 200 years after its publication: *Manuale Tipografico* by master designer, punchcutter, printer, Giambattista Bodoni (1740–1813).

"Printing is the final outcome of man's most beautiful, ingenious and useful invention: that I mean, of writing. . . ." wrote Bodoni in the preface to his posthumously published *Manuale*.[17] He did perfect writing during his time, creating a family of letterforms that were a reaction against the mannered and floriated letters in vogue in the 18th century. Bodoni's type design aesthetic was one of verticality, fine serifs, high contrast in weight, with lines set in open leading and opulent margins, and printed smooth white paper. The *Modern Roman* or *Didone* typeface classification was born as a result of his work, which consequently was appropriated by the mid-20th-century Modernist school of graphic design.

The two-volume *Manuale* included the best examples of Bodoni's oeuvre in type design: 276 different faces in various sizes, including alphabets for several languages and typographic ornaments. Published in a small edition of only 290 copies on handmade paper, it was as much a fine-press book as a type specimen, and sent to many sovereign courts of Europe on behalf of the book's patron, the Italian Duke of Parma for whom Bodoni spent his career printing. It's invaluable that the Cary Collection holds two copies of the *Manuale*. Each copy shows different binding styles and was connected to a "celebrity" of typographic history. Jackson Burke, the type director of Merganthaler Linotype Company, owned one copy, and the second was purchased in 1977 to mark the tenure of the Collection's founding curator, Alexander Lawson.

---

17   Giambattista Bodoni, H.V. Marrot, trans. "Preface to the *Manuale Tipografico* of 1818," *Bodoni: Printer of Parma*. Rochester: The Press of the Good Mountain, 1971, 49.

CHROMATIC WOOD TYPE

Specimens of Chromatic Wood Type, Borders, Etc. Manufactured by Wm. H. Page & Co.
Greeneville, CT.: The Co., 1874.

Nineteenth-century America experienced the boom of the Industrial
Revolution and through it, factory production of everyday goods. More
products on the market drove up sales competition, and hence print
advertising flourished in volume: newspaper ads, leaflets, posters, and
billboards. Large display typography ruled the era—shouting out pitches
in bold, ornamented, or huge letters. Wood type (relief characters carved
from maple blocks, rather than cast from metal) printed these dynamic ads.
During wood type's heyday in the late 19th century, some 20,000 wood
typefaces were estimated to be on the market.

William H. Page (1829–1906), of Connecticut, emerged by the 1860s
as the country's chief producer of wood type. The Page Company had an
extensive catalog of original character designs, intricate borders, and tint
blocks cut with exacting precision. Page even patented a new process of
creating wood type by die stamping instead of mechanical routing, thereby
decreasing production times. Intense rivalry through the mid-1880s with J.
E. Hamilton's cheaper veneered types sent Page's market share into decline.
He sold his business in 1891 to the Hamilton Manufacturing Company of
Two Rivers, Wisconsin.

The Page Company's typographic legacy is sealed, however, in this
magnum opus, which design historian Rob Roy Kelly wrote, "has been
rightfully acclaimed as containing the most superb wood type specimens
ever printed."[18] *Specimens of Chromatic Wood Type* is a tome of 100 plates
of Page's fantastic character designs printed in up to seven colors each—
sometimes with metallic inks, and always with interesting overprinted
hues. Each page is vibrant in its mastery, pushing the limits of creative
advertising through letterpress in perfect registration and a light kiss
impression. Only ten copies of this rare specimen are known to exist in
libraries nationwide.

---

18   Rob Roy Kelly, *American Wood Type: 1828–1900; Notes on the Evolution of
     Decorated and Large Types* (New York: Da Capo Press, 1977), 73.

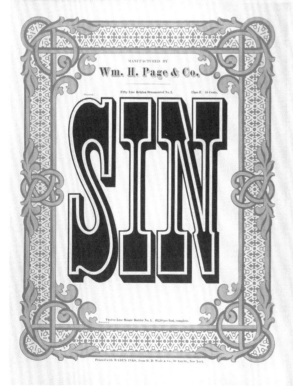

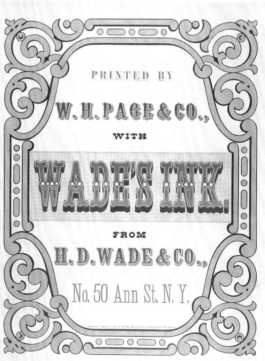

A NURSERYMAN'S PLATE BOOK

A.H. Chadbourne & Co. *Flower and Flowering Shrub Seed Peddler's Plate Map with 45 Color Plates*. Rochester, NY, ca. 1890.

Graphic communication has always incorporated color as a form of expression, a way to enhance an image, or a means to capture naturally occurring phenomena. The methods of reproducing color in print have traced a long journey of scientific and technical advancements, which are well documented in the Cary through printers' manuals, specimens of printing processes, and even texts on the physics of light and the chemistry of ink pigments. The nineteenth century saw the proliferation of different color graphic reproduction processes—in which printers in Rochester, New York, contributed some innovations.

The hearty climate and rich soil of the Genesee Valley, combined with the ease of 19th-century transportation routes via canal and railroad, created the perfect opportunity for Rochester to become a leading center for plant nurseries. A supporting industry of color printing firms rose quickly in our "Flower City" to meet the demand for advertising materials to sell these seeds and plants.[19] The floral pictures shown here come from a "nurseryman's plate book," a kind of catalog which was first developed by Rochester printer D. M. Dewey in the 1850s. These were color prints that were bound together in a small leather book that could be easily slipped into a traveling salesman's pocket. The images were often printed through creative mixtures of different layered processes: engravings for the outlines, chromolithography for fields of color, stencil or pochoir printing for subtle gradients, and hand-coloring for finishing details.[20] The resulting pictures of fruit, flowers, and ornamental plants are irresistibly vibrant, and so effective in understanding the aesthetic values and consumerism of this era of American history.

---

19   Karl S. Kabelac. "Nineteenth Century Rochester Fruit and Flower Plates," *University of Rochester Library Bulletin*, Volume 35, (1982), 93–114.

20   David Pankow. "Seed Money in the Flower City; The Art and Technique of Horticultural Illustration in Rochester, 1840–1940," Exhibition co-sponsored by Memorial Art Gallery at the University of Rochester and RIT Cary Graphic Arts Collection, 1988.

Perpetual Clematis, Henryii.

A strong growing, vigorous variety, producing flowers of large size, fine form, and in color beautiful creamy white. Blooms profusely from July to October.

J. W. THOMPSON & CO.

CLEMATIS JACKMANII.

This is perhaps the best known of all the newer, finer perpetual Clematis. The plant is free in its growth, and an abundant and successional bloomer, producing flowers until frozen up. The flowers are large, of an intense violet purple, remarkable for its velvety richness. Either in the open ground as bedding plants, or plants for rock work, or covering for verandahs none could be surpassed.

Clematis, Lawsoniana.

This is one of the finest of all, and should find a place in every collection. It is a vigorous grower, remarkably free and continuous bloomer, beginning with the earliest and holding on with the latest. The flowers are very large, often six inches in diameter. Opening a rich pleasing rosy purple, they change to a lighter purple. Commencing an earliest protuse success corresponding in any able for its velvety richness. June to October.

J. W. THOMPSON & CO.

AMPELOPSIS VEITCHII.

A beautiful climbing plant, introduced from Japan, resembling somewhat our Virginia creeper, but of finer foliage and more beautiful appearance; and adhering more perfectly to a wall or building; will cover wall or trellis without any training or fastening. The foliage is a dense mass of bright glossy green in summer, turning to crimson scarlet of every shade and hue during the autumn, at which time it is most grandly beautiful. It is perfectly hardy, and requires no protection. FRUIT AND FLOWER PLATES.

J. W. THOMPSON & CO., ROCHESTER, N. Y.

Chinese Wistaria.

A very beautiful climbing plant. Attains an immense size, growing at the rate of 15 to 20 feet in a season. Foliage and flower very attractive. Perfectly hardy.

J. W. THOMPSON & CO.

Chinese Wistaria.

A very beautiful climbing plant. Attains an immense size, growing at the rate of 15 to 20 feet in a season. Foliage and flower very attractive. Perfect

J. W. THOMPSON & CO'S., COLORED PLATES, ROCHESTER, N. Y.

VARIEGATED LEAVED.

Corana Magnolia Variegata.

KELMSCOTT/GOUDY PRINTING PRESS

Albion Press No. 6551. Hopkinson & Cope, 1891.

In January 2014 the Cary Collection welcomed an extraordinary addition to our Arthur M Lowenthal Memorial Pressroom. A few months earlier, Christie's in New York announced that it would be auctioning the printing press that was used by William Morris, the father of the Arts and Crafts movement in England. Late in his career Morris founded the Kelmscott Press and produced books of the highest standards of design, papermaking, and printing. His masterpiece is *The Works of Geoffrey Chaucer* (1896) known more commonly as simply the Kelmscott Chaucer. It is a book so beautiful that it is considered one of the finest ever printed. The printing press that Morris used to print his edition of Chaucer was the very press being auctioned at Christie's—Hopkinson & Cope No. 6551.

The Kelmscott printing press had been on the Cary Collection's desiderata list for some time, not only because of its legacy with Morris, but for the impressive history that followed. In 1924, the press left England and traveled to Marlborough, New York to the print shop of Frederic Goudy. Shortly thereafter, Goudy sold the press to Spencer Kellogg Jr. who ran the Aries Press of Eden, New York, a suburb of Buffalo. In 1932, the press then moved to New York City where it was owned by the Cary Collection's namesake, Melbert B. Cary Jr. Following Cary's death in 1941, it was bequeathed to his pressman George Van Vechten. In 1960, J. Ben and Elizabeth Lieberman acquired the press for their Herity Press and topped the press with a Liberty Bell, a reminder of the vital role that private presses play in the freedom of the press.

On December 6, 2013, the Cary Collection had the good fortune of being the highest bidder at the Christie's auction. The purchase was made possible by the generous support of the Brooks Bower family. Bower, a 1974 graduate of the School of Print Media, is an RIT trustee and chairman and chief executive officer of Papercone Corp., an envelope-manufacturing firm in Louisville, Kentucky.

Photo by John Myers.

THE KELMSCOTT CHAUCER

Geoffrey Chaucer. *The Works of Geoffrey Chaucer, Now Newly Imprinted, Edited by F.S. Ellis; Ornamented with Pictures Designed by Sir Edward Burne-Jones, and Engraved on Wood by W.H. Hooper*. Hammersmith, Middlesex.
Printed by William Morris at the Kelmscott Press, 1896.

The introduction to the *Canterbury Tales* in the Kelmscott Press's *Works of Geoffrey Chaucer* is considered one of the most beautiful page openings ever printed in a book. Its power comes from a stunning combination of late medieval and early renaissance aesthetics, and those of the late Victorian period. The "Chaucer" typeface created for the publication was inspired by the gothic typefaces used in the 15th century by Peter Schöffer (page 56). The wood-engraved illustrations designed by Edward Burne-Jones reflect the Pre-Raphaelite art popular at that time.

Cary Professor Alexander Lawson acquired this copy of the Kelmscott Chaucer for the Cary Collection around 1971 as an exemplar of outstanding fine press printing. The Cary Collection's copy also features a striking blind-tooled maroon morocco binding by English bookbindery Riviere & Son.

INCUNABULA

Johannes Marchesinus. *Mammotrectus super Bibliam*. Mainz, Peter Schöffer, 1470.

Books printed in the first half-century following Gutenberg's invention of printing in Europe are referred to as incunabula, Latin for "in the cradle." Thus, these books represent printing practices when the art was still in its infancy and conventions were still being established. Incunabula are books in transition. For example, they often lack title pages and page numbers, components of books that would take time to become established norms. Moreover, borrowing from manuscripts, illustrative details in the earliest printed books were often supplied by hand.

The Cary Collection has a selection of exemplars from the incunabula period, the oldest being *Mammotrectus super Bibliam* (Nourish upon the Bible) dating to 1470. The book is a grammatical guide to the Bible written by the 14th-century Italian friar, Johannes Marchesinus. Its printer, Peter Schöffer, started his career as a young apprentice to Johann Gutenberg and his partner Johann Fust. In fact, Schöffer might have worked on the Gutenberg Bible.[21] Schöffer's edition of *Mammotrectus super Bibliam* is shown in classes at the Cary Collection not only as an example of early European printing, but also as a specimen of the early gothic typeface used by Schöffer that would inspire future type design, including the Chaucer typeface created for William Morris' 1896 edition of *The Works of Geoffrey Chaucer* (page 54). Shown in the detail is Schöffer's printer's device, a logo used to identify the printer.

---

21   Christopher De Hamel, "The Gutenberg Bible," *The Book:*
     A History of the Bible (London; New York: Phaidon, 2001), 199,
     and *Gutenberg, Man of the Millennium: From a Secret Enterprise*
     to the First Media Revolution (Mainz : City of Mainz, 2000), 74–78.

THE CAPITALS FROM THE TRAJAN COLUMN

Frederic W. Goudy. Alphabet Wood Engraving Blocks For *The Capitals from the Trajan Column at Rome*. New York: Oxford University Press, 1936.

Although the triumphal column dedicated to the Roman emperor Trajan was completed in 113 CE, the inscription at its base has been inspiring students of lettering for millennia. The characters in this text are thought to be some of the most perfectly wrought examples of inscriptional capitals of the Latin alphabet. They have served as models for many analog types of the past, cast in metal, and now as digital typefaces.

American master of type design Frederic Goudy (1865–1947) designed a typeface after these letters in 1930. Goudy also published *The Capitals from the Trajan Column* as a meditation on the Trajan letterforms. It is a slim volume illustrated with drawings of each extant letter, and his interpretations of those characters not present in the inscription or even yet in the Latin alphabet of the first century, such as J and U. Goudy offered astute analyses of their swells, upright strokes, and serif construction—praising above all— their beautiful simplicity.

Jo Shifrin and Jethro K. Lieberman recently donated Goudy's original wood blocks carved for this edition to the Cary Collection in honor of Elizabeth and J. Ben Lieberman, who preserved them at their private printshop, The Herity Press. The blocks join a rich collection of Goudyiana at the Cary, that is, works by Goudy and his talented wife, Bertha. These include rare cases of type and standing type forms, typecasting equipment, presses he owned, manuscripts by his biographers, unpublished photographs, voluminous correspondence, drawings and lettering, and of course his many prints, type specimens, and books. The variety of material and the uniqueness of its artifacts make it one of the finest Goudy collections in the country.

BRUCE ROGERS' CENTAUR

Museum Capitals typeface matrices.

Typeface design by Bruce Rogers; Engraved by Robert Wiebking in 1914.

Moulds for alphabets in 12, 20, 24, 30, 48, and 60 point sizes.

Typophiles today may treasure a case of vintage metal letterpress type, as it is a dwindling commodity that can be newly manufactured only by a handful of extant hobbyist type founders. The ability to cast new type relies partly on access to matrices of the characters—the punched or engraved moulds, which can be filled repeatedly with a molten alloy of lead. Matrices are essentially the *negatives* of a metal typeface, and hold the same importance as the source from which innumerable fonts can be replicated. The Cary Collection holds several typographic matrix collections, including the matrices for arguably the most important American roman typeface to have been designed in the early 20th century— those of Bruce Rogers' Museum Capitals, a design that was later called Centaur.

Bruce Rogers (1870–1957), was a virtuoso book designer who advanced the practice of "allusive typography," in which "the design alludes to, or even quotes from, some historic style."[22] He designed hundreds of books, and one superlative allusive typeface in Centaur. The 15th-century types of Venetian printer Nicolas Jenson inspired Rogers. He perfected the drawings of his letterforms over photographic enlargements of Jenson's 1470 edition of the Roman historian Eusebius, making thoughtful improvements in balancing weight and serif structure for contemporary production.

Henry Watson Kent, director of the Metropolitan Museum of Art's in-house print shop, purchased the exclusive rights to the typeface's capitals in 1914 and had matrices cut in several sizes. A savvy designer, Rogers retained the right to use the full upper- and lowercase font in his own projects. The first time the full face appeared in print was in *The Centaur*, a slender book of romantic prose published by the Montague Press in 1915. Monotype later released Centaur fonts for public use in 1929.

In the 1980s, the matrices for six sizes of Museum Capitals came into the Cary Collection when curator Herbert Johnson acquired the archive of Huxley House, which was a fine printer for the Met. By that time, the Met's printing establishment had long closed, and its materials had been scattered. In 2012, the Dale Guild Type Foundry recast the 20-point Capitals from the Cary's mats, selling new Centaur type almost 100 years after its first inception.

---

22 Frederic Warde. "On the Work of Bruce Rogers," *The Fleuron, A Journal of Typography.* London, 1925.

TYPE

A B C D E F G H I J ?

&

K L M N O P Q U R , -

SCENTAUR

S

1 2 3 4 5 6 7 8 9 0 &

BR

FOR THE VOICE

El Lissitzky, Vladimir Mayakovsky. *Dlja Golosa*.
Berlin: RSFSR Gosudarstvennoe Izdatel'stvo, 1923. Edition: 2,000–3,000. 18.7 × 12.5 cm

Dlja Golosa (*For the Voice*) is the collaborative tour-de-force between the
Russian poet Vladimir Mayakovsky (1893–1930) and artist Lazar Markovich
Lissitzky (1890–1941) containing an anthology of the thirteen most popular
poems of Mayakovsky's revolutionary spirit with typographic illustrations
by Lissitzky. The poems were written from 1913 to 1922 and appeared pre-
viously in newspapers and journals of the era. Mayakovsky approached Lissitzky to enter into the partnership in Berlin where many Russian expatri-
ates were living and creating artistic work. Lissitzky's visual poems provide
a dynamic interchange with the written texts. Lissitzky described his vision
for the book in *Typographic Facts*:

> This book of poems by Mayakovsky is meant to be read aloud. To
> make it easier for the reader to find any particular poem, I use an
> alphabetical index. The book is created with the resources of the
> compositor's type-case alone. The possibilities of two-colour printing
> (overlays, cross-hatching and so on) have been exploited to the full.
> My pages stand in much the same relationship to the poems as an
> accompanying piano to a violin. Just as the poet in his poem unites
> concept and sound, I have tried to create an equivalent unity using
> the poem and typography. [23]

The poems are printed in a nearly pocket-sized volume with the innovative thumb index providing a visual and typographic key to the poems. *For
the Voice* was published in Berlin by the Soviet State Publishing House, RSFSR
Gosudarstvennoe Izdatel'stvo. However, Lissitzky worked with a German
printer by instructing him to employ only, as Lissitzky states, elements from
the type-case in unusual and inventive ways. The illustrations are bold and
dynamic and are meant to incite the viewer to read the poems aloud—to the
point of shouting—as Mayakovsky did to excite his audience into action!
The page-spread seen here depicts the beginning stanza of first poem "Left
March—To the Sailors" which sets the book into lively motion. The unification
of verse and typography makes *For the Voice*, one of the quintessential exemplars of Russian Constructivist book design.

---

23   El Lissitzky, in *Gutenberg Feschrift*, 1925, translated in Sophie Lissitzky-Küppers.
      El Lissitzky. Life. Letters, Texts, intro H. Read, trans. Helene Aldwinckle and Mary
      Whittal (London: Thames and Hudson, 1968), 95.

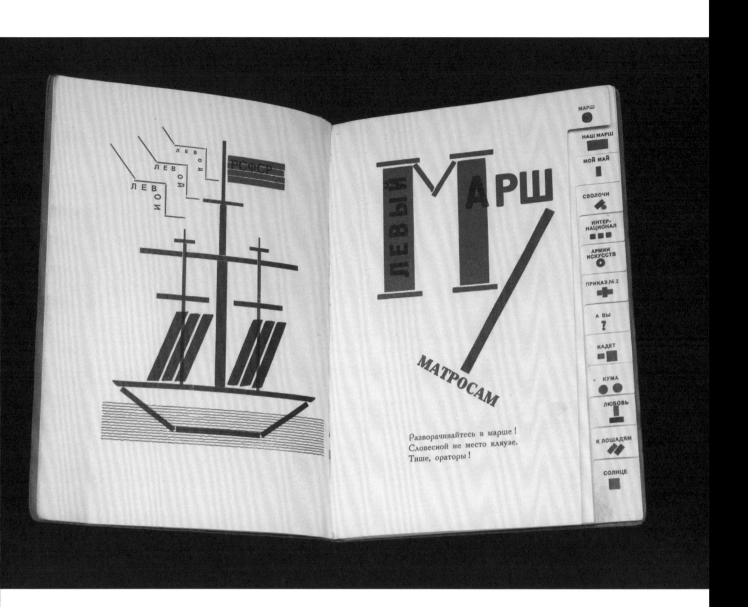

THE BOLTED BOOK

Fortunato Depero. *Depero Futurista, 1913–1927*. Milano; Parigi:
Edizione della Dinamo, 1927.

One of the most exciting areas of growth in the Cary Collection is our collection of avant-garde typography. We are acquiring samples of innovative type design from the 1920s and '30s in reaction to the interests of faculty in RIT's School of Design. Examples of the avant-garde also complement our Graphic Design Archive, revealing the strong influence of this experimental era on Modernist design of the 1950s and '60s.

An outstanding revolutionary avant-garde piece is *Depero Futurista* by Fortunato Depero (1892–1960). This book is one of the most important exemplars of the Italian Futurist Movement and one of the centerpieces of 20th-century avant-garde typography. Depero's typographic experimentation pushed the boundaries of graphic design, showing how text on the page could be made to suggest motion, machinery, and architecture.

Depero Futurista is perhaps best known for its industrial bolted binding, a feature of the book that has earned it the nickname the Bolted Book. While the design is not particularly functional and makes the book difficult to operate and preserve, it is one of the most visually arresting bindings of its time.

65

CRANACH PRESS HAMLET

William Shakespeare. *The Tragedie of Hamlet, Prince of Denmark.*
Weimar: Cranach Press, 1930.

Considered one of the "milestones in twentieth-century private printing" and a "classic of private-press book production," Count Harry Kessler's editions of *Hamlet* exemplify the finest execution of all aspects of book-making.[24] He first published a German translation, *Die tragische Geschichte von Hamlet Prinzen von Daenemark* in 1928 and later, an English companion in 1930. These editions were a collaboration between many of the period's greatest book artists. Edward Gordon Craig, the celebrated actor, theatre director, and wood-engraver, brought his personal experiences with Shakespeare's *Hamlet* to his design of the book's evocative illustrations. Calligrapher Edward Johnston designed a black-letter typeface reminiscent of fifteenth-century printers such as Johann Fust and Peter Schöffer. Eric Gill produced the lettering found on the title and half-title pages, as well as the title page's illustration. Harry Gage-Cole executed the printing, demonstrating "the ability of the pressman at its best."[25] Finally, Otto Dorfner bound copies of the Cranach *Hamlet* in various striking styles.

The culmination of these efforts resulted in one of the most outstanding representations of a Shakespearean work ever printed. As book historian Roderick Cave once observed, "Of all private presswork in the Kelmscott tradition, the Cranach *Hamlet* is the greatest."[26]

---

24 Lindsay Newman, "From Stage to Page: *Hamlet* with Edward Gordon Craig." *The Book as a Work of Art: The Cranach Press of Count Harry Kessler.* Ed. John Dieter Brinks (Laubach: Triton, 2005), and James Hamilton, 'Craig, (Edward Henry) Gordon (1872–1966)', *Oxford Dictionary of National Biography,* Oxford University Press, 2004; online edn, May 2008. [http://www.oxforddnb.com/view/article/32608, accessed 20 March 2013].

25 Roderick Cave, *The Private Press* (New York: R.R. Bowker, 1983), 146.

26 Ibid.

SAXONIS GRAMMATICI
HISTORIÆ LIBER TERTIUS

HORVENDILLUS ET FENGO,
QVORUM PATER GERVEN
DILLUS, JUTORUM PRAE
FECTUS EXTITERAT EIDEM
A RORICO IN JUTIÆ PRAE
SIDIUM SUBROGANTUR.
AT HORVENDILLUS, TRIEN
NIO TYRANNIDE GESTA,
PER SUMMAM RERUM GLO
RIAM PIRATICAE INCU
BUERAT, CUM REX NOR
VAGIAE COLLERUS, OPE
RUM EJUS AC FAMAE MAG
NITUDINEM AEMULATUS
DECORUM SIBI FORE EXIS
TIMAVIT, SI TAM LATE
PATENTEM PIRATAE FUL
GOREM SUPERIOR ARMIS
OBSCURARE QVIVISSET.

Cujus classem varia fretum navigatione scrutatus offendit. Insula erat medio sita pelago, quam piratae collatis utrinquesecus navigiis obtinebant. Invitabat duces jucunda littorum species, hortabaturexterior locorum amoenitas interiora nemorum verna perspicere lusvarum indaginem pererrare. Ubi forte Collerum Horvendillumque invicem sine arbitris obvios incessus reddidit. Tunc Horvendillus prior regem percontari nisus, quo pugnae genere decernere libeat, praestantissimum affirmans, quod paucissimorum viribus ederetur. Duellum siquidem ad capessendam fortitudinis palmam omni certaminis genere efficacius fore, quod propria virtute subnixum, alienae manus opem excluderet. Tam fortem juvenis sententiam admirans Collerus, cum mihi, inquit, pugnae delectum permiseris, maxime utendum judico, quae tumultuationis expers duorum optram capit. Sane et audacior et victoriae promptior aestimatur. In hoc communis sententia est, hoc ultro judicio convenimus. At quoniam exitus in dubio manet, invicem humanitati deferendum est, nec adeo ingeniis indulgendum, ut extrema negligantur officia. Odium in animis est; adsit tamen pietas, quae rigori demum opportuna succedat. Nam etsi mentium nos discrimina separant, naturae tamen jura conciliant. Horum quippe consortio jungimur, quantuscunque animos livor dissociet. Haec itaque pietatis nobis conditio sit, ut victum victor inferiis prosequatur. His enim suprema humanitatis officia inesse constat, quae nemo pius abhorruit. Utraque acies id munus, rigore deposito, concorditer

DIE TRAGISCHE GESCHICHTE VON
HELSINGØR EINE TERRASSE VOR DEM SCHLOSSE

Bernardo
Francisco   Wer da?
Halt! wer seid ihr?   Nein, ihr steht mit rede.
Bern. Lang lebe der könig!
Franc. Bernardo?
Bern. Er.
Franc. Ihr kommt gewissenhaft auf eure stunde.
Bern. Schlag zwölf. Pack dich zu bett, Francisco.
Franc. Dank für die ablösung! 's ist bitter kalt,
    Und ich bin kränklich.
Bern. War eure wache ruhig?
Franc. Alles mausestill.
Bern. Schön, gute nacht!
    Wenn ihr auf meine wachtgefährten stoßt,
    Horatio und Marcellus, heißt sie eilen.
        Horatio und Marcellus treten auf.

HAMLET PRINZEN VON DÆNEMARK

Franc. Ich denk, ich höre sie. – He! halt! wer da?
Hor. Freund dieses bodens.
Mar. Und des königs lehnsmann.
Fran. Habt gute nacht!
Mar. So tretet ab, kam'rad.
    Wer hat euch abgelöst?
Fran. Bernardo steht auf posten.
    Nochmals gut nacht!
Mar. Holla, Bernardo!
Bern. Sagt, ist Horatio hier?
Hor. Ein stück von ihm.
Bern. Grüß gott, Horatio! grüß gott, Marcellus.
Hor. Nun, ging das ding auch heute wieder um?
Bern. Die wacht war ruhig, wie Francisco sagt.
Bern. Horatio glaubt an nichts, nennt hirngespinst
Mar. Das fürchterliche schreckbild, das wir sahn.
    Und darum hab ich selbst ihn hergebracht,
    Damit der augenschein ihn überzeuge
    Und seinen zweifel tilge. Mag er dann,
    Wo's wiederkehrt, mit dem gespenste reden.
Hor. Pah, pah! Es wird nicht kommen!
Bern. Setzt euch denn,
    Und lasst uns nochmals euer ohr bestürmen,
    Das so verschanzt ist gegen den bericht,
    Von dem, was wir gesehn.
Hor. Gut, sitzen wir,
    Und laßt Bernardo, was er weiß, erzählen.

LE CINQVIESME LI
VRE DES HISTOI
RES TRAGIQVES,
LE SUCCEZ & EVE
NEMENT DESQVEL
LES EST POUR LA
PLUS PART RE
CUEILLY DES CHO
SES ADVENUES DE
NOSTRE TEMPS
ET MIS

ET LE RESTE DES HISTOIRES ANCIENNES. LE TOUT FAICT ILLUSTRÉ ET MIS EN ORDRE, PAR FRANÇOIS DE BELLEFOREST COMINGEOIS. A LYON PAR BENOIST RIGAUD MDLXXXI · AVEC QVELLE RUSE AMLETH, QVI DEPUIS FUT ROY DE DANNEMARCH, VENGEA LA MORT DE SON PÈRE HORWENDILLE, OCCIS PAR FENGON SON FRÈRE, ETAUTRE OCCURENCE DE SON HISTOIRE

Quoy que j'eusse délibéré des le commencement de ce mien oeuvre de ne m'esloigner, tant peu soit, des histoires de nostre temps, y ayant assez de sujets pleins de succez tragiques, si est-ce que partie pour ne pouvoir en discourir sans chatouiller plusieurs plusieurs digne d'estre offert à la noblesse Françoise, partie aussi que l'argument que j'ay en main m'a semblé digne d'estre offert à peu esgaré mon cours de ce siecle, et sortant de France et pays voisins, suis allé visiter l'histoire Danoise, afin qu'elle puisse servir et d'exemple de vertu, et de contentement aux nostres,

MULTIMEDIA *MACBETH*

William Shakespeare. *Macbeth*. Edited by A.R. Braunmuller;
commentary by David S. Rodes. New York: Voyager, c. 1994.

Cary curators sometimes refer to the library's holdings as "tablet to tablet,"
alluding to the long evolution that connects cuneiform clay tablets to
modern mobile devices. Although a large portion of the library's artifacts
connects with the past, the Cary Collection is just as concerned with inves-
tigating the present and looking to the future. Over the past three decades,
the nature of the book has changed dramatically, and the Cary Collection
works to document these transformations by acquiring material such as
tablet computers, e-readers, and e-books.

Today, reading digital books is fairly commonplace. Although it
might seem like a relatively recent phenomenon, e-books in various
formats date back to the mid-20th century. Founded in 1984, the Voyager
Company was an early innovator of books on CD-ROM. The Cary owns
a copy of their edition of Shakespeare's *Macbeth*. Released in 1994, this
electronic edition offered a rich multimedia experience. In addition to
traditional textual components like annotations, collation (comparison of
the texts used in early editions) and a concordance, the playtext is en-
riched with features like clips of famous film adaptions, a photo gallery
of both historical and modern resources, and an audio recording of a
performance by the Royal Shakespeare Company. Looking back across
the relatively short distance of twenty years, it is clear that the publication of the Voyager *Macbeth* is an important moment in the history of
book publishing, although perhaps a fleeting one. Not long after, similar
multimedia editions shifted from CD-ROM to the Internet on sites such
as *Internet Shakespeare Editions*.[27] The Voyager *Macbeth* is also a testament
to the ways in which the works of Shakespeare have been frequently the
subject of innovations in book publishing.

---

27   *Internet Shakespeare Editions*, http://internetshakespeare.uvic.ca.

Macbeth and the Witches (4.1 – the show of kings), from the first illustrated edition of Shakespeare's works, edited by Rowe (1709).

DISPOSABLE DADA

Marcel Duchamp. *Dada 1916–1923*. New York: Sidney Janis Gallery, 1953.
94.5 × 61.0 cm.

The poster that Marcel Duchamp designed to be the catalog for his 1953
Dada retrospective exhibition has become a major collector's item, although its creator might not have intended it to be so. According to Carroll
Janis, the son of gallery owner Sidney Janis, "When the painstakingly
produced catalogue was finally received, Duchamp, as it has been reported,
took a sheet in his hands, crushed it into a loose ball, and suggested that a
trash can full of these paper balls be offered to visitors entering the vernis-
sage."[28] Perhaps many took Duchamp's cue, because a relatively small
number of the catalogs survive.

The copies that weren't balled up and tossed into the trash testify to
Duchamp's design masterpiece. Numbered exhibition items descend and
rise out of the upper right and lower left corners. In the center are four
descending essays by Jean Arp, Tristan Tzara, Richard Huelsenbeck, and
Jacques Levesque, each jagged column distinguished from the others by
its typeface. Printed over the text are the exhibition title and a "DADA"
border in a style and color that reflects the avant-garde typography of the
1920s and '30s (page 62).

---

28   Carroll Janis, "Marcel Duchamp Curates Dada." *Art in America*
     (June–July 2006), 215.

70

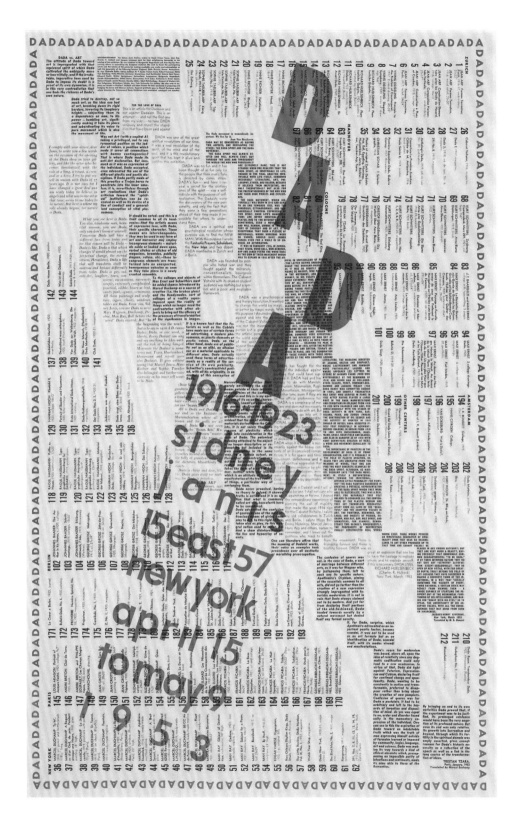

LAPIDARY INSCRIPTIONS

Eric Gill, Inscriptional Alphabet, Hoptonwood stone, 1938, 45 × 57 cm.
Commissioned by George Grady through Paul Standard.

In a library filled with paper, it may be surprising to find some of the
Cary's most prominently displayed artifacts are derived from stone:
plaques cut in slate and limestone by the masters Edward Catich, Eric Gill,
Christopher Stinehour, and those of the John Stevens Shop. But the history
of letterforms has its foundation in painted and carved inscriptions that
have lasted millennia on this most durable of substrates.

Flanking our door is a rubbing of the inscription at the base of the
Roman Emperor Trajan's triumphal marble column, dated 113 CE. These
chiseled capital letters have been the models for countless manuscript
hands and later, metal and digital typefaces. Every young RIT student of
typography sees this rubbing in a class. The goal of this exposure is that
the capitals will inspire, as they certainly did designer Eric Gill (1882–1940),
who could view the same inscription as a plaster cast at the Victoria &
Albert Museum in London.[29]

From humble beginnings in cutting gravestone lettering, Eric Gill built
a prolific career as an illustrator, calligrapher, and type designer. Today
Gill is best known for his eponymous sans serif typeface, Gill Sans, but he
never strayed far from his preferred medium of stone. He was praised as,
". . . one of the greatest sculptors of our day [who] is also the creator of the
purest inscriptional lettering done since the Renaissance, and . . . the first
lettering able to rival, rather than cleverly imitating, the free originality
of the inscriptions of ancient Rome."[30] Accordingly, the characters on the
Cary's Gill Alphabet Stone certainly echo the monumentality of the Trajan
Column, but they take a light turn in color and curve—a fresh interpretation on an ancient genre.

---

29 Eric Gill, *An Essay on Typography* (London: J. M. Dent & Sons, Ltd., 1931,
     reprint 1960), 28.

30 Beatrice Warde writing as Paul Beaujon. "Eric Gill: Sculptor of Letters," *Fleuron*
     7, Garden City, NY: Doubleday & Dorian, 1930.

an A B C
DEFGHIJKL
bcdefghijklmopqrs
MNOPQRST
tuvwxyz 123456789
UVWXY&Z
EG 1938

"BY EVERY LOVER OF LETTERFORMS"

Correspondence from Edward Johnston to Paul Standard, 26 April–5 May 1944.
Paul Standard Papers.

Cary certainly holds large collections of books and printing artifacts, but at least half of the vaults are filled with diverse archival collections. These consist of the personal papers of designers and calligraphers, as well as the corporate records of type foundries and publishing houses. In all, these collections are so valuable because they document the ideation and process work that has gone into the creation of some of the finest Western design of the past two centuries. The Paul Standard Papers represent such an archive and contain the letters, writings, books, and ephemera collected by Paul Standard (1896–1992), a calligrapher and author who promoted chancery or italic handwriting in the early 20th century.

Standard was well connected in the field of book arts, and his correspondence collection at Cary shows it—some 57 boxes of letters received! One of his most prized possessions was this letter from Edward Johnston (1872–1944). In 1943, Standard and a colleague from Chicago took up a charity collection for Johnston who was on the brink of destitution as a result of poor health and the strapped war economy. They did this as humble tribute to Johnston who wrote the landmark book *Writing, Illuminating & Lettering*, 1906. Johnston's work in examining ancient manuscripts and teaching a generation of students had revived calligraphy as the basis for all letterforms, by hand or in print. Johnston also was instrumental in refining the shape of twentieth century sans serif typefaces, as he designed the font for the London Underground metro service, and most importantly, was the long-time mentor of Eric Gill.

Paul Standard solicited over $1,600 for the Edward Johnston fund from a veritable *Who's Who* of more than 120 people in the book world including Bruce Rogers, Frederic Goudy, Fritz Kredel, Dard Hunter, Victor Hammer, Alfred Knopf, Harry N. Abrams, Random House, and Monotype Company. He sent these funds to Johnston, (valued today at about $20,000), with a note that read "...we tender you our small gift as a token of a long-standing debt owed you by every lover of letterforms." Johnston's masterful calligraphic thank-you note was written on his lap whilst bedridden, and so astounded Standard that he had always hoped to reproduce it for wider appreciation. After the Standard Collection came to Cary, this letter was finally published in the book *Thinking in Script; A Letter of Thanks...ca.* 1995.

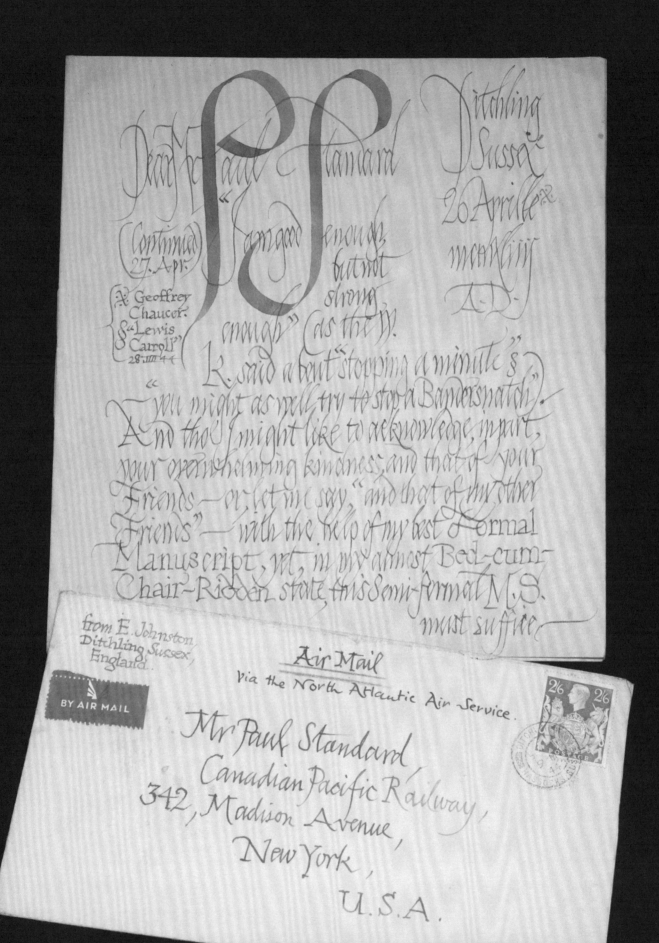

Dear Mr Paul Standard

Ditchling Sussex
26 Aprile '42
MCMXLIII
A.D.

(Continued)
27. Apr.

X Geoffrey
Chaucer.
§ "Lewis
Carroll"
28.IIII.4 <

"I am good enough, but not strong enough" (as the W.

K. said about "stopping a minute"):
" you might as well try to stop a Bandersnatch). —
And tho' I might like to acknowledge, in part,
your overwhelming kindness, and that of your
Friends — or, let me say, "and that of my other
Friends" — with the help of my best Formal
Manuscript, yet, in my almost Bed-cum-
Chair-Ridden state, this Semi-formal M.S.
must suffice —

from E. Johnston,
Ditchling Sussex,
England.

BY AIR MAIL

<u>Air Mail</u>
Via the North Atlantic Air Service.

Mr Paul Standard
Canadian Pacific Railway,
342, Madison Avenue,
New York,
U.S.A.

2/6   2/6

A MODERN TYPOGRAPHIC MASTER

Hermann Zapf. *Manuale Typographicum*. Frankfurt, Z-Presse: 1968.
Working layouts and correspondence for the production of this book.

From 1977 to 1987, RIT faculty counted a maestro in its ranks, while
establishing an enduring relationship with one of the most influential type
designers of the 20th century. Hermann Zapf, (b. 1918), who received the
RIT School of Printing's first Frederic W. Goudy Award in 1969 for excel-
lence in typography,[31] was invited back to teach typographic computer
programming, which at that time was the only position of its kind in the
world.[32] Zapf is one of those rare individuals whose versatile talent for
calligraphy and book design extends to type design. He mastered analog
typeface production early in his career at the Stempel Type Foundry in
Germany. He went on to harness and even improve the changing technology through the metal, photographic, and digital eras. His repertoire
includes such ubiquitous typefaces as Palatino, Optima, and Zapfino.

While at RIT, Zapf taught using the extensive holdings of the Cary
Collection as exemplars for his students. He also donated generously to
the library, making it one of two repository archives for his work—the
other in Wolfenbüttel, Germany. Among all of Zapf's books, broadsides,
and manuscripts here, a large collection of hand-drawn layouts for both
the 1954 and 1968 editions of *Manuale Typographicum* demonstrates his
virtuosity in working with type. The later edition was ambitiously subti-
tled, "100 Typographical Arrangements with Considerations about Types,
Typography and the Art of Printing, Selected from Past and Present,
Printed in Eighteen Languages." Any student who sees these unique
materials cannot help but marvel at the meticulous thought and skill that
Zapf put into the design of each page.

---

31   Mark F. Guldin et al. *Twenty Years of the Frederic W. Goudy Award.*
      Rochester: Press of the Good Mountain, 1988.

32   *From the Hand of Hermann Zapf.* Washington: Washington Calligraphers
      Guild, 1993.

Varje

Varje tidsperiod har präglat sitt eget uttryckssätt i de olika konst-
grenarna – så också i bokstävernas utformning. Den som känner
till bokstävernas avhängighetsförhållande och förändringar väntar
sig att dagens livsyttringar och formtänkande också avspeglas i de
bokstäver som skapas för en tidsmässig typografi.   *Erik Lindegren*

JONATHAN AND PATRICIA ENGLAND COLLECTION

Margaret Kaufman and Claire Van Vliet. *Aunt Sallie's Lament*. Altered.
Vt.: Janus Press, 2004. Edition of 120. 29 cm.

Janus Press began in 1955 and is named after the ancient Roman god of beginnings and transitions. Janus is often depicted with two faces—one looking backward to the past and one looking forward—and perfectly embodies the vision of the Press's founder, Claire Van Vliet. Awarded a John D. and Catherine T. MacArthur Foundation Fellowship in 1989, Van Vliet excels at a bookmaking style that pays homage to the fine press traditions of the past while creating innovative books that look to the future. Claire Van Vliet sees herself as the "orchestrator" of Janus Press which counts on many artisans involved in a true creative, collaborative endeavor.[33]

Aunt Sallie's Lament is part of the Jonathan and Patricia England Collection of American Fine Printing. Patricia England, an extraordinary collector of fine press and artists' books, donated over seven hundred books to the Cary Graphic Arts Collection in 1991. Another portion of the England collection was donated to the National Gallery of Art. Patricia England acquired Janus Press titles with vigor, and there are over twenty Janus press titles in the collection.

Aunt Sallie's Lament illustrates a poem by Margaret Kaufman, a remembrance by a Southern quilter of a poignant life and a love lost. Several versions of *Aunt Sallie's Lament* exist. The first, published in 1988, is quite spare in color and was followed by a trade edition published by Chronicle Press in 1993. In the 2004 version shown here, Claire Van Vliet and her team experimented with more color and complicated woven paper structures including Japanese and handmade paper. A number of structural elements and paper from the Chronicle Press version were also incorporated. *Aunt Sallie's Lament* is a symphony of color, collage and woven paper and highlights the quilting leitmotif that occurs in several other Janus Press titles.

Claire Van Vliet celebrates the creative and intimate possibilities of the book. In 2013, she remarked, "When people look at art on the wall they are afraid they are going to be judged on what they say about it . . . But when they open a book, they open themselves."[34]

---

33 Candace Page. "Meet Claire Van Vliet: A Paper Pioneer in the Northeast Kingdom." *Burlington Free Press,* March 2, 2013. http://archive. burlingtonfreepress.com/article/20130303/ARTS/303030002/Meet-Claire-Van-Vliet-A-paper-pioneer-in-the-Northeast-Kingdom

34 Ibid.

ACKNOWLEDGMENTS

Special thanks to:

Steven Albahari
Bruce Austin
Brooks Bower
Shirley Bower
Molly Cort
Heather Engel
Patricia England
Vincent FitzGerald
Seth Gottlieb
Thanh Hoang
Herb Johnson
Derek Joyce
Paul Kellar
Elizabeth Lamark
Barry Moser
Mary Flagler Cary Charitable Trust
Bernard C. Middleton
David Pankow
Zahra Partovi
R. Roger Remington
Jethro Lieberman and Jo Shifrin
Marnie Soom
Jason Stryker
Claire Van Vliet
Lynn Wild
Lili Wronker
Hermann Zapf

COLOPHON

Typefaces: Palatino Linotype and Optima Nova

Design: Marnie Soom

Printing and binding: Complemar Partners, Inc., Rochester, NY

Paper: International Paper Accent Opaque